DREAMS

I'm Never Gonna See

The Takeover of

and Other Essays

Brian Lee Knopp

Author of *Mayhem in Mayberry:*
Misadventures of a P.I. in Southern Appalachia

To the memory of Timothy Andrew "The Ace" Boylan
August 23, 1960 – August 29, 2023

We are still laughing ... through the tears.

Final Cover + Book Design: Susan Rhew Design, Asheville, NC
Printing + Binding: IngramSpark, La Vergne, TN
Fonts: Adobe Caslon Pro, Franklin Gothic and Cooper Black

Cosmic Pigbite Press

1070-1 Tunnel Road
#10-276
Asheville NC 28805
cosmicpigbitepress@gmail.com

Table of Contents

Dreams I'm Never Gonna See: The Takeover of WDIZ Rock 100/FM

The fading Polaroid was proof of the shocking incident from the past. But when I found the photo, I felt no shock.

There was the posturing young man with the dark assault rifle and bundle of explosives. Black cloth obscured his features. Only his eyes shone forth, burning with malevolent intent.

All the familiar features were there. The photo should have triggered outrage toward this terrorist. At the very least, it should have expanded the growing numbness that comes from diminished expectations for our species.

It did neither. After a moment of recollection, it made me laugh.

Talk about the Imp of the Perverse!

Because the rifle was fake. The explosives were phonies—a pair of wooden nunchucks wrapped in stereo speaker wire and taped to a dead 9-volt battery.

And the so-called terrorist was me.

On August 6, 1981, five members of the Ida Lupino Liberation Organization (ILLO) took control of WDIZ, central Florida's Home of Rock and, at the time, one of the nation's hottest radio stations. They forced DJ Mick Dolan off the air, disconnected the phone lines, and gathered all the station staff into one room to hear the ILLO's demands. A shaken Dolan would later describe the intruders over the airwaves:

> "Well, it's been an interesting afternoon here at the station for the WDIZ Amateur Hour contest. Some Rock-n-Roll Commandos from DeLand stopped by ... ."

1

But neither Dolan nor then-program director Bob Church would ever mention in public what really went down. They didn't disclose the details of the stealth invasion of the Southland Building—which housed WDIZ and, ominously enough, a US Marines recruiting office. Nor did they tell how the Rock-n-Roll Commandos made their getaway through Orlando rush hour traffic by commandeering a POS Plymouth Fire Arrow.

The ILLO's direct-action campaign never surfaced again. Their righteous demands were lost to history, rendered superfluous by the dumbing down effect that corporate media takeovers would have on the best rock stations in the country.

DEMAND ONE: WE WANT TO BE ON THE WDIZ ROCK 100 AMATEUR DJ HOUR!

DEMAND TWO: NEVER EVER PLAY THAT ANNOYING ALE 8 COMMERCIAL AGAIN!

DEMAND THREE: DINNER FOR FIVE MEMBERS OF OUR ORGANIZATION AT THE BEEFY KING!

DEMAND FOUR ...

The true identities of the ILLO members—Thing One and Thing Two, The Rock, The Ace, and Charlie the Tuna—have never been revealed. Until now.

PART ONE

Children of the Sun

In 1994, the comedy film *Airheads* popularized the legend of lovable losers taking over a radio station to promote their cause.

But thirteen years *earlier*, five dudes from DeLand, Florida had done just that.

On August 6, 1981, members of the Ida Lupino Liberation Organization (ILLO) took WDIZ Rock 100-Orlando hostage. And got away with it.

I was one of them. We did it on a workday, in the sweltering heat of a dog day afternoon in central Florida. We did it without firing a shot, without hurting anyone, and without being arrested.

Nostalgia often blurs the most vivid recollections. Unlike other forms of hindsight, it is subject to frequent correction and, at times, outright rejection. In fact, there seems to be an obligatory disclaimer tacked onto even the most earnest retrospectives on recklessness: "You couldn't get away with that nowadays. Don't even try."

But that disclaimer totally misses the point. Because back in the 1980s, it was a truth generally acknowledged—even in Florida, where weirdos did and do thrive like so many overheated bugs—that hijacking a federally-licensed radio station would damn sure get you in BIG trouble.

Attacks on radio stations have always been dangerously provocative. Recall that the Second World War started with the takeover of a German radio station. Hitler justified his invasion of Poland in 1939 because of a "false flag" assault on the Gleiwitz radio station staged by German troops wearing Polish Army uniforms.

So, no disclaimers or trigger warnings are necessary.

What I'd like to reexamine, then, is not why the 1981 WDIZ takeover should not or could not be carried out today. Rather, I want to focus on why it seemed so attractive—necessary, even—for me to have participated in something so breathtakingly stupid in the first place.

In the parlance of our times, the issue was radicalization. What influenced the ILLO to feel imbued with a special purpose, and to regard the stunt as irresistibly sublime? The mitigating factors of clinical insanity, mental retardation, or mind-altering substances do not apply here, as I will attempt to show.

Asked more directly: What made me and my comrades—Thing Two, The Rock, The Ace, and Charlie the Tuna—do what we did?

We were swayed by time and place, of course. The gritty, anarchic Seventies were still convulsing against the affectations and phony moralism of the Eighties. We were part of the huge shock wave of winter-weary economic refugees that struck the Sunshine State in the Seventies. The ranks of our fellow travelers were riddled with misfits, malcontents, military brats, lost children of tradesmen, dubious dreamers, and scamacious schemers.

Going West meant having a reliable car and navigation skills. Going South required only that you submit to gravity and wear cheap sunglasses.

Central Florida back then wasn't so much a melting pot as it was a cheap fondue set for funpigs simmering in their own excesses and seeking the redemption and validation they couldn't get elsewhere. Amidst the white sand beaches, dense pine forests, fragrant orange groves, sprawling cattle ranches, tacky tourist traps, and lake-spotted landscape, old grievances

and incompatible ideologies rotted or washed away. New ones took their place. There was disco to defeat, blue-collar jobs to protect, gas shortages to endure, drug money to resist. The world of men struggled against the burgeoning world of mice who took their orders from a micromanaged Magic Kingdom.

To most of the young adults who flocked to the state, outrageousness and obscenity were better alternatives than passivity and anonymity. Central Florida was the perfect place to fight for and enjoy those alternatives.

All the ingredients for spontaneous combustion were there. But it was the soundtrack to it all that made the mayhem so memorable— and so worthwhile. There was an unmistakable calling at the time, an exalted energy that emerged from Northern Rust Belt heavy metal being hammered onto Southern blues rock. We wrapped ourselves in the sound. Wore it as a suit of sonic armor. Embraced it as a tireless lover.

No one who experienced the central Florida music scene from 1975– 1985 could remain a mere mortal for long. The true believers became Children of the Sun. They glowed brighter than neon flamingos. They breathed in pure jasmine and breathed out the erotic scent of Hawaiian

Tropic suntan oil. In the sticky heat that lasted through the night, They pulled excitement out of the sky. Lightning flashed from Their eyes and burned desire into hard purpose. Troubles were transitory. Defeat was for lesser creatures.

I was a True Believer. So were the other members of the ILLO. The musicians of the time were our gods. For a little bit of coin and a lot of worship, they, in turn, made us feel godlike and blameless, too.

In the summer of 1981, the hammer of the gods in central Florida was WDIZ.

For an eternal seven minutes on Hiroshima Day, the ILLO would wield that hammer.

PART TWO

Rock-n-Roll Party
in the Streets

Between 1975–1985, the central Florida music scene was hotter than the mean-assed sun burning down on its outdoor concerts. At night, it cooked in the sultry darkness of its many rock clubs. Homegrown talents— Tom Petty, Allman Brothers, Lynyrd Skynyrd, Molly Hatchet, Blackfoot, .38 Special, The Outlaws—jammed head-to-head with the best music acts from across the USA and beyond. The greater Orlando area was a rich constellation of fabled music venues. The Great Southern Music Hall. The Lakeland Civic Center. Brassy's in Cocoa Beach. Fern Park Station, with its funky fermenting sticky floor. The Joint in the Woods, a cavernous barn featuring an always-mutilated punching bag hanging from the ceiling in the men's room. Year after year of stellar lineups for the huge Rock Super Bowls held in the Tangerine Bowl.

Make no mistake. The Music wasn't just another recreational drug. It wasn't mere diversion. The Music was direction. It was destiny.

It is impossible to overstate the influence The Music had on the lives of the True Believers. And we were multitudes. We were everywhere. Almost half of my high school's 2000-plus students cut class on October 21, 1977, the day after the airplane crash in Mississippi that killed three members of Lynyrd Skynyrd and severely injured the rest of the band.

We were a force to be reckoned with. Or at least we were after 10 AM or thereabouts.

The nonstop rock-n-roll party in the streets didn't need justification. It only needed participation and promotion. The True Believers provided the former. The rock radio stations provided the latter.

In the beginning, there was WORJ-FM 107. The radio's very call letters suggested "ORGY". And for a glorious while, that's what the station delivered: All the sex, drugs, and rock-n-roll your ears could stand. WORJ or "Zeta 7," as it was usually called, was the subversive little ole Mt. Dora radio station with true underground roots that reached back to the early 70s.

But tragedy struck Zeta 7. The repercussions that followed had a very long reach. You can still see upside down Zeta 7 license plates cruising around Florida today, sported by drivers who weren't even alive back in February 1981. That's when WORJ changed overnight from a kickass rock station to a bowel-blocking easy listening format. But somehow these folks felt the loss, all the same. Like feeling the phantom pain coming from a severed limb. Hanging the inverted tag is their way to support the original protest, honor the first protesters, and in their own way, piss back at the corporate gods for their transgressions against rock-n-roll.

Before I blame WDIZ, in general, and DJ Mick Dolan, in particular, for inciting a band of True Believers into disrupting the radio station in mid-broadcast—please keep in mind the fate of Zeta 7 … and the point I made earlier about how provocative radio station takeovers are.

Upside down Zeta 7 license plate

WDIZ. The station's call letters were a play upon DIZney World. That cutesy marketing ploy should have crippled the rock station in its infancy. But it didn't. WORJ's loss was WDIZ's gain. The Rock 100 grew up quickly to be Godzilla, slaying all other rock station monsters. It dominated rock radio in the 80s throughout the Southeast, if not throughout the country.

They say imitation is the sincerest form of flattery. Copycat stations sure flattered the hell out of WDIZ's playlists. They stole the morning show "The Rude Awakening." Imitators muddled through the concepts of "shock jocks" and "fine-line funny" which had first been perfected by Alan Baxter and Mark Samansky, the stars of WDIZ's "Baxter and Mark Show."

But imitations are usually limitations. The imitators were reductions of the true innovators and risk-takers. Like Russian nesting dolls, they were little figurines fitting neatly inside their own derivative programming, never really breaking out and touching the very souls of their audience.

The greatest rock stations were not conformists. The best DJs were not ripoff artists. Nor were they robots relying on predictable song rotations to deliver the so-called "real" music of cash registers ringing up advertising dollars. No, they constantly upped the ante, urging their listeners onward— possibly to the point of no return.

Any DJ with even the slightest pretension toward greatness knew this to be true.

Like Mick Dolan, for instance.

Dolan was the station's promotions manager and weekday afternoon DJ. He is remembered by his fans for his "Five at Five" weekday playlist that raucously announced that the workday was over, commencing countdown to party.

When he was on the air, Dolan didn't rant, rave, break things, or rely on racy innuendos. He had a soothing, mellow delivery with just a hint of Midwest flatlands. He sounded like an earnest but hip high school guidance counselor. His calming voice was an odd counterbalance to the scorching message coming from his turntables. But with his creation of the Rock 100 Amateur Hour contest, the station's new imperative for wildness was Marshall amp loud, up-the-neck Fender guitar clear.

Dolan repeatedly reminded his listeners that to win the weekly guest DJ slot, contestants had to be off the chain. He challenged the faithful to do something zany, something unforgettable, something dedicated to—and, ultimately, deserving of—the wildly-creative central Florida rock scene over which WDIZ presided.

Thing One, Thing Two, The Rock, The Ace, Charlie the Tuna—heard the call. We took up the challenge. We delivered the goods.

Twice, in fact.

PART THREE

Bad Company

Two weeks before the assault on the radio station, ILLO won the coveted WDIZ Amateur Hour slot. We did it by packaging and shipping a real live person to the radio station. But even that accomplishment didn't satisfy us.

Because it didn't satisfy Mick Dolan.

He complained on the air for days afterwards that the Amateur Hour contest had become pretty lame ever since some guy had won by mailing himself to the station.

"We want something crazy. Something completely original and memorable."

There were reputations at stake, all the way around. Mick Dolan had to pimp the rising star status of WDIZ as *the* rock station to beat. He dared the True Believers to preserve the central Florida legacy of batshit-crazy rock-n-rollers, and to prove their devotion by competing for the Amateur Hour in the wildest manner possible.

The ILLO would have to outdo themselves.

The Ida Lupino Liberation Organization wasn't a political faction or paramilitary group. It wasn't a gang. It wasn't even a true direct-action organization with bylaws, member initiations, recruitment, statement of purpose, etc. It had none of those things. For three friends and two brothers, it was part joke, part inspiration.

The Rock had come up with the name. He was obsessed with Ida Lupino, the actress considered by many to be the Queen of the B-movies. She was an inescapable feature of late night TV back in the 70s and 80s. Her omnipresence deeply affected him. In turn, he infected the rest of us with his monomania for her as a subversive deity deserving our utmost devotion.

Ida Lupino was an unlikely mascot for young blue-collar males running amok in central Florida at a particularly auspicious time to do so. But her mythic status as the under-appreciated, unstoppable underdog of the silver screen was one we eventually aspired to attain. Her divinity became even more apparent to us whenever we combined malt liquor and Krispy Kreme donuts in truly staggering proportions.

It was exhilarating to scream out her name in the steaming Florida night while we rocketed toward "O-ville" at twice the speed limit, in search of sonic sustenance for the soul. On such frenzied outings, shouting "IDA LUPINO!" sounded more like "I LOVE LIBIDO!" Which could have been the war cry for twenty-somethings like us everywhere.

For us, the Ida Lupino Liberation Organization had a strong—though admittedly indefensible—appeal. If nothing else, it gave us an enigmatic acronym to stencil in big black letters

**SENDER: THE I.L.L.O. FRAGILE! THIS SIDE UP!
DO NOT CRUSH, FOLD, SPINDLE, or MUTILATE!**

on a shipping label we taped to the huge refrigerator box.

The box which we hand-delivered to the Southland Building.

The box containing The Rock, our friend and ILLO founder.

The Rock was our unanimous choice for the special delivery guest DJ. He was tall, strong, good-looking, Brooklyn brash and, if need be, Brooklyn tough. He owned the largest collection of rock albums and memorabilia of anyone we knew. He was renowned in high school for wearing a different rock concert t-shirt for every day of a given school year, and for wearing a Cheap Trick bowtie and Rolling Stones lips on his graduation gown.

The Rock was his namesake because he was cool, solid, reliable under fire. That is, until you gave him a strawberry Yoo-Hoo to drink. Then all bets were off. Yoo-hoo transformed him in the same predictably unpredictable way that playing "Pop Goes the Weasel" did for Curly of the Three Stooges fame. Most importantly, however, The Rock was too tough to get claustrophobic, or suffer heat stroke from being sealed in a cardboard box for over an hour in July in central Florida.

The Ace played the role of package delivery driver. He was a nondescript person who had several personalities. And none of them got along very well. Yet he used them all to his advantage as a dedicated prankster.

The Ace was miraculously exempt from many laws of the land, including those governing cause-and-effect. He was like a cartoon character, the meek mouse who could pull a rocket from his pocket and blast off to safety just as the cat closed in. Folks tended to overlook him because he blended seamlessly into the background of legitimate jobbers, deliverymen, mall store clerks, paying customers, rightful ticketholders, et al.

That is, until he chose not to blend in.

By then, it was too late.

His victims realized—with rising panic—that whoever he was, and whatever he was doing, had suddenly become surreal, much too close, and completely unnerving.

There are far too many appalling Ace anecdotes to list here. But The Night of the Living Bowling Trophy always comes to mind.

One night The Ace showed up uninvited and virtually naked to a hotel party. He was wrapped head-to-toe in aluminum foil and carried a silver bowling ball. He walked all stiff and crinkly into a corner of the room and struck the pose of the figurine mounted atop a bowling trophy.

The Rock and Thing One   The Ace (Bowling Trophy) and Friend

Despite all the inquiries and provocations from the party guests, he never said a word. Because he couldn't. He didn't move for almost an hour. Then he fell over in a faint from heat exhaustion caused by the aluminum foil. But he never let go of the bowling ball. Not even when the paramedics arrived.

We could count on The Ace to go the distance.

He came up with a UPS "Big Brown" delivery driver uniform somehow. Which was key, of course. He could always whip out stuff like that. In times of need, he was the "ace" card up our collective sleeve.

We wanted The Rock to look like he had lived in the refrigerator box for a couple of shipping days. We told him to be unshaven and unkempt, which was the hardest part of the gig for him, appearance-conscious as he was. We placed discarded fast food containers and empty Yoo-Hoo bottles in the box for added realism.

The job of adding realism to foolish fun—and vice versa—was shared between my twin brother and myself, a.k.a. Thing Two and Thing One. Don't fixate on those nicknames. The aliases were transient. We had plenty more. We went by Buckwheat and Alfalfa for a spell, spray-painting these names on every water tower we could climb in the area. No one was the wiser. No one knew who was who, or which was which, anyway.

Since we had rarely been identified correctly throughout our lives, we didn't place much stock in names or titles. And since identical twins were the original victims of collective punishment—the innocent punished along with the guilty for convenience's sake—we didn't place much stock in the consequences to our feats of derring-do, either.

What we did care about was living an unconventional and incomparable life.

More than money or prestige, we wanted to push the limits, beat the odds, defy all doubters, and have fun doing so, for as long as we could. We wanted to make our lives into a living work of magic realism, complete with a killer soundtrack. And if that soundtrack encouraged dirty deeds done dirt cheap, so be it.

Thing One   Thing Two and Friend

While the ILLO had no one true leader, nothing succeeds like excess enthusiasm. Which my brother and I supplied in abundance. We also had a certain innate flair for tag-team persuasion. We were very successful at convincing reluctant yet like-minded others of the importance of carrying out complex shenanigans without getting bogged down in morale-sucking vagaries like career goals or clean criminal records.

The special delivery of The Rock went off without a hitch. After several radio station staffers gathered to inspect the giant package The Ace had wheeled in on a mover's dolly, The Rock burst forth from the cardboard container. Popping up like a human Jack-in-the Box, he shouted that he wanted to be the guest DJ. After their initial shock wore off, the staff collapsed into laughter. Then they told The Rock that he was the week's winner right then and there.

One of the members of ILLO did not take part in the special delivery DJ caper. But he would play a crucial role in the assault on the radio station.

Charlie the Tuna was ILLO's style manager and Captain of Cool. He showed us how to dress right and dance right and make all the right moves with women.

His nickname came from the old Starkist Tuna commercials—"Sorry, Charlie … Starkist doesn't want tunas with good taste. Starkist wants tunas that taste good!" I gave him the nickname as a mild protest. He was

Charlie the Tuna

always so poised, always the smooth operator. He had such good taste in the finer things in life. Whereas I was the most socially inept and style-indifferent member of the group. It took him weeks to patiently wean me off my bad social habits, such as circumventing certain nightclub dress codes by folding napkins in the shape of a shirt collar and tucking them inside the neck of my pocket t-shirt.

When confronted by one of my fashion horror shows, Charlie would look me over slowly head to toe. Then he'd shove his hands in his front pockets, and shake his head toward the sky and sigh.

"You're not gonna meet any fine-looking women that way. You're only gonna meet the badass bouncers."

He was absolutely right. He was always right about those things.

Of the five of us, Charlie the Tuna probably knew best how to navigate uncharted social waters. His quiet confidence and brilliant smile generally won over any resistance. In stressful situations, though, he would stutter. Yet his verbal faltering was more endearing than debilitating. It disarmed suspicious strangers and gave him even more situational leverage, as folks were moved to help this handsome polite young man with a speech impediment.

For precisely those reasons, we used Charlie the Tuna as the frontman for the assault on WDIZ.

PART FOUR

Breaking the Law

"ARE YOU GUYS OUT OF YOUR FUCKING MINDS?"

That's what Bob Church, WDIZ's program director, repeatedly screamed over the phone, minutes after we had carried out the successful takeover of his radio station.

He was furious. The conversation was awkward, to say the least.

"YOU KNOW WHY YOU GUYS AREN'T IN JAIL ALREADY? ONE REASON. BECAUSE WE DON'T WANT IT TO GET OUT HOW EASY IT WAS FOR FOUR GUYS TO WALK IN AND TAKE OVER A FEDERALLY-LICENSED RADIO STATION!"

Bob Church was right about one thing. The August 6, 1981 takeover of WDIZ by the Ida Lupino Liberation Organization was easy.

We planned the operation during the forty-minute drive to the station. We were already familiar with the Southland Building and the Lee Road area of Orlando. We had to hit the station while Mick Dolan was on the air in the afternoon. Which was a tricky time slot for the ILLO, because of our respective work schedules. Frantic last-minute maneuvers and lame excuses to bosses won the day.

Transportation—the getaway car—also turned out to be a problem. The Rock's Lemon Twist '71 Challenger was too easy to spot in traffic. Thing Two's '69 Chevelle had been totaled weeks earlier, rear-ended by a drunk driver. Thing One refused to volunteer his Mom's '76 Malibu Classic, for obvious reasons. Charlie the Tuna had no car.

That left The Ace's '79 Plymouth Fire Arrow.

Much has been written about the crap cars forced upon us by Detroit from the mid-Seventies to the mid-Eighties. But the Fire Arrow was truly the product of an evil genius and the perfect vehicle for a prankster like The Ace. Because it was a practical joke on wheels. A cleverly-disguised practical joke. Somewhere underneath the idiotic racing stripes and garish graphics was supposedly a Japanese motor, touted for its reliability and pep.

Not in this car.

Although The Ace's sled resembled a sporty-looking ride, it couldn't go over 60 mph without catching fire, or travel more than 100 miles from home without breaking down. Or without the silly factory-installed antitheft alarm blaring out unbidden and staying on until the battery was disconnected.

It was an 80-mile round trip from DeLand to Orlando. That was uncomfortably close to the Fire Arrow's maximum safe cruising range. And you couldn't merge onto I-4 rush hour traffic in Orlando unless your vehicle could do at least 70 mph in a quarter mile. Which The Ace's poky piece of shit couldn't do unless it was strapped to a NASA rocket.

Worse, The Ace's car was almost as identifiable as The Rock's. It was a two-door hatchback that could barely contain five crammed men and their radio station assault accessories. The Ace relied excessively upon his sister's hairspray to mask the smells of burning motor oil and overheating electrical circuits that permeated the interior. We were glued to the sticky seats and to each other. We had to ride the whole way with the windows down in the August heat. We smelled like Aqua-Net.

But the spirit of Ida Lupino smiled down upon us that day. We were convinced that we would succeed, Fire Arrow be damned. And we hoped that Ida Lupino would protect us from a chance encounter with the US Marine recruiting office located in the Southland Building along with WDIZ.

Our plan was simple. The Ace would remain in the Fire Arrow, parked as close to busy Lee Road as possible. Charlie the Tuna would go into the station first, alone. He would buy enough time for The Rock to enter the building from a different entrance than that used by Thing One and Thing Two, who would have to hide in a stairwell to put on their disguises.

The Rock would carry a guitar case in which the two toy machine guns and fake explosives were hidden. While Charlie the Tuna was stammering his way into the heart of whomever was talking with him, The Rock would walk right up to the DJ booth unobserved and get Mick Dolan's attention. Then on a verbal cue, Thing One and Thing Two would emerge from hiding and rush the station. The Rock would open the guitar case, distribute the weapons, and the takeover would commence.

Our plan worked. With some surprises, of course. As could be expected with this kind of operation.

For starters, Charlie the Tuna didn't stutter. Not one word. We had counted on the stress of invading a radio station to provoke several precious minutes of repeated consonants and labored pronunciations. Instead, he entered the station and spoke as loudly and clearly as Tim Curry in *The Rocky Horror Picture Show*. The receptionist understood him perfectly. Which meant he ran out of bogus things to say. Which meant the receptionist became suspicious, and called out for assistance.

He just stood there in his mirrored shades, blue Hawaiian shirt and white disco pants, beaming his megawatt smile, saying nothing further.

When The Rock entered the station, several staff members were already circling the curiosity that was Charlie the Tuna. The staffers immediately swung their heads toward The Rock striding through the entrance.

There was a tense standoff. Undaunted, The Rock kept walking toward Mick Dolan, who was inside the DJ's booth.

"Can we help you?"

"Yeah, remember me? I was the guest DJ two weeks ago. I just need to talk with Mick for a sec."

"I'm sorry, but he's on the air right now. You'll have to wait."

"THAT'S NOT GOOD ENOUGH."

Thing One and Thing Two barely heard their cue. We had black shirts over our heads and black cloth over our faces, after all. And we were lurking in a concrete stairwell down the hall. Plus, at that precise moment, two uniformed Marines started up the stairs toward us. They were talking about—of all things!—the Iran hostage crisis, which had been resolved in January of that year.

Several agonizing seconds of indecision passed. Then Thing One and Thing Two bolted up the stairs and burst into the station. There, The Rock opened the guitar case, tossed them the phony guns, and kept the dummy bomb for himself.

He noted the "ON THE AIR" light glowing through the glass. He opened the sound booth door, and brandished the phony explosives at Dolan.

"MICK! YOU'RE COMING WITH US!"

After a few beats, Dolan spoke.

"I guess I have no choice."

Thing One and Thing Two began rounding up the employees and unplugging phone lines as they went through the office.

Thing Two had been a DJ in college. He knew that dead air from a radio station was an FCC no-no. He told The Rock to make sure Dolan cued up a record which would play on the air for the entire time the ILLO planned on being in the station.

"Put on Boston's Foreplay/Long Time!"

That song would give us seven minutes to make our demands and our getaway.

Dolan and his fellow staffers were wide-eyed but quiet. They looked shut down. They moved like sleepwalkers. Only the receptionist looked visibly nervous, licking her lips and flicking her eyes over us and around the room.

The Rock declared our demands.

"WE ARE THE IDA LUPINO LIBERATION ORGANIZATION! AND HERE ARE OUR DEMANDS!

DEMAND ONE: WE WANT TO BE ON THE WDIZ ROCK 100 AMATEUR DJ HOUR!

DEMAND TWO: NEVER EVER PLAY THAT ANNOYING ALE 8 COMMERCIAL AGAIN!

DEMAND THREE: DINNER FOR FIVE MEMBERS OF OUR ORGANIZATION AT THE BEEFY KING!

DEMAND FOUR ...”

At the mention of the B-movie queen and the Amateur Hour contest, Dolan and one or two other staffers visibly sagged with relief. They started muttering and shaking their heads.

“Aw, shit … unbelievable … Jesus Christ!”

But the rest remained still as statues. Right up until we left the station. The Rock continued.

“Don’t call us. We’ll call you to confirm your decision about the Amateur DJ Hour!”

We dumped the fake weapons back in the guitar case and raced out of the station in two separate groups. The Rock and Charlie the Tuna ran out the front. Thing One and Thing Two ran out the back, pulling off our disguises as we fled. We jumped into the Fire Arrow.

But the Fire Arrow wouldn’t start.

The Ace had not kept the motor running, as we had planned. He knew from bitter experience, however, that prolonged idling would cause the radiator to boil over and the engine to vapor lock. He took a chance on the dodgy alternator and timid starter. And they let him down.

Incoherent swearing swirled around the car. Then absolute silence, punctuated only by the sick hiccupping of the invalid engine.

It was Charlie the Tuna who called down the Goddess.

“IDA LUPINO!”

The Fire Arrow spluttered to smoky stinky life.

On our way back to DeLand, The Ace had the car stereo tuned to WDIZ. Mick Dolan came on the air, and had this to say about our adventure:

“Well, it’s been an interesting afternoon here at the station for the WDIZ Amateur Hour contest. Some Rock-n-Roll Commandos from DeLand stopped by … .”

We rejoiced.

"IDA! IDA! IDA!"

We pulled into a 7-Eleven store to use the payphone. The Rock called the radio station. He introduced himself as a member of the ILLO. Bob Church immediately cut in on the line when he heard who was calling.

"ARE YOU GUYS OUT OF YOUR FUCKING MINDS?!"

"No. We want to be on the Amateur DJ Hour."

"NO SHIT? YOU KNOW WHY YOU GUYS AREN'T IN JAIL ALREADY? ONE REASON. BECAUSE WE DON'T WANT IT TO GET OUT HOW EASY IT WAS FOR FOUR GUYS TO WALK IN AND TAKE OVER A FEDERALLY-LICENSED RADIO STATION."

"Hey, it's your fault. You dared us to be wild and crazy. To do something memorable. Don't blame us. Mick Dolan used me on the air as one of the examples. He said 'Some guys mailed a DJ in a cardboard box a week ago.' That was us!"

Church hung up the phone.

Thing Two offered to call the station. After all, it was my brother and I who had wanted to share the guest DJ slot for that week. He spoke with Dolan. Who was more reasonable than Church, if not necessarily more forgiving. Thing Two gave him our real names and home phone number.

Bob Church promptly called our home. My mom answered.

CHURCH: "Are these boys crazy? Do I need to call the police?"

MOM: "Yes, all boys their age are crazy. No need to call the police on them, though. Goodbye."

The radio station picked some guy from Apopka for that week's guest DJ. I think the dude sent in a stuffed and mounted fish with WDIZ bumper stickers on it. Or some damn forgettable thing like that.

On August 8, Thing Two sent a letter to the station, pouring out our devotion as True Believers.

Yes, we feel good that we went through with our risky plan to demonstrate our earnest desire to get on the airwaves. Brian and I have lived here for seven years. We've always tuned you guys in. But it was not until we left for colleges in the North that we really appreciated "The Rock" of central Florida. After 9 months of rigid rock programming, pre-taped intros and outros, and straightjacketed tune selection ranges, it does our hearts good to come home and jam to a triple shot or miniconcert .... . We know we're home when we can pick up DIZ on I-75. We associate DIZ with our way of life here. We would like to play a small part in furthering that association by being guest DJs, as a way of saying 'thank you' to you, to the bands, and to our friends and fellow partyers all over this area .... .

Thing Two even offered a list of alternative—and legal—schemes that Mick Dolan could announce over the air if they chose us. Like sending them a poster bearing the outline of a Flying V guitar, with the guitar's body comprised of glued guitar picks, a light bulb mounted on the guitar's headstock, and golden glitter letters on the neck reading "Turn us on Sunday, Mick!"

We wanted so badly to be guest DJs.

The postscript to the letter read "LONG LIVE IDA LUPINO!"

There was no reply.

8/8/81

Mick Dolan
WDIZ Amateur Hour
100.3 FM
Airwaves, Fl.

Mick, (and Mr. Church, ~~or whoever~~ considered some guy from Apopka over us,
even though the guy didn't even <u>write</u> to you),

Hello, remember us? We visited your offices last Thursday to ask
you, in person, to be on the Amateur Hour. Despite some rough edges,
I feel our presentation was quite good. With all our fellow "commandoes"
(your own term, Mick) working all day, it is quite difficult to run home,
get one's camouflage attire on, and hold up a radio station, unrehearsed.
I thought are number was far superior to all of the other "crazy stunts"
pulled in order to be on the Amateur Hour. 25 pounds of rock magazines,
cookies, cakes, groovy letters--all seem to pale in comparison to our
little "plea". Brian and I wanted it that way, Mick, you, yourself, have
been imploring the listeners to "do something, don't just write",and you
have stressed the "craziness" requisite to spinning the wax up in the booth.

Brian and I "did" something. And, yes, we are crazy enough to
rock that studio like it hasn't been rocked in a while (and, of course,
couldn't be rocked, what with your programming requirements and all). But
we are <u>not</u> of the lunacy that it would be unsafe or unwise for you to permit
us on the Amateur Hour. We are not deranged, but, then again, if I were to
lie to you and say we are complete whitebreads who took off their Izods for
one afternoon to take over your studio, I would be insulting your own
flamboyance, and selling ourselves extremely short. We are interesting
people.

Yes, I feel good that we went through with our rather risky plan to
demonstrate our earnest desire to get on the air, Brian and I have lived
here for 7 years. We've always tuned you guys in, but it was not until we
left for colleges in the North that we really appreciated "The Rock" of C. Florida.
No bullshit. After 9 mos. of rigid rock programming, with pre-taped intros
and outros and straightjacketed selection ranges, it does our hearts good to
come home and jam to a "triple shot" or miniconcert. When Brian and I cruise
home for the summer, or for vacations, we know we are home when we can pick
you up on I-75. We associate DIZ with the life here. We would like to take
a small part in that association, as a kind of "thank you" to our friends
and partyers all over this area for staying still while we are gone.

So, you see, our desire to be on the air is ardent, but <u>stable</u>. Our
imaginations are practically unlimited, but we are not insensitive to your
caution in announcing our deed over the air. The world is full of clods and
malcontents who carry their emulation of real trendsetters to the realm of
the bizarre. Look at all the jerks who tried to leap gorges on Hondas, trying
to be Evel Knievel, not to mention the number of green-hued youngsters who
get messed up, annually, trying to go through walls or bust stuff like the
Hulk. I've seen some of my friends mess up trying to do some of the other
stuff we've dreamed up over the years. It's a shame people lack prudence and
self-restraint, but there it is. You're right, Mick. If you announced we had
you guys at gunpoint, some PCP-laden wacko would bust in your place and try
to kill you with the jagged remnant of a broken Velvet Underground album, or
somethin'. Our number, I think, preserved a careful balance between terror and
good clean fun. Our successors would probably just be twisted, or vulgar.

Hence, in compliance with your request, here are some suggestions for
"substitutee antics" that you can say, over the air, that we did to get on
the Amateur Hour. They're not hell-fire, but it's really tough for me to
think of something crazy to do that no nut could blow out of proportion

24

1. Brian and I catch you outside the parking lot of Southland. We are dressed as Superheroes, Thor, and Aquaman. I threaten you that if we are not placed on the Amateur Hour, I will level the building with my mystic hammer, Mjolnar. Brian merely adds that he will command legions of spiny lobsters to rise up out of the sea and surround you all. Worse, they will be inedible spiny lobsters (egad!)

2. Inspired by Judas Priest new album, we arrive at your office as "Solar Angels", complete with wings, halos, and electric guitars. We offer you and all the staff salvation if you let us on the Hour. (I like this one, we plan to do it anyway, at our next hotel party. You should come. Youll die.)

3. We send our letter on posterboard, upon which has been mounted a Flying V guitar, made out of melted guitar picks. One light bulb is mounted by the "bridge" of the guitar. Beside it are the words "turn us on Sunday, Mick!"

4. We send you 100 3 oz bottles of D-4 Discwasher, telling you to "get the hint" and allow us on. This is dumb idea, but no dumber than some of the others I've heard on the air, and, besides, if people copy this one you'll never have to buy that expensive shit again.

There, 4 safe, non-toxic, non-flammable ideas for stunts we could haved done, but didn't, cuz we're not rich, good with paste and scissors, or because we liked the one we really did, better. They're still different, too. One of these "substitutes", together with the energy of our real stunt, should, I hope, satisfy you. This is a deliberatly long letter, Mick, I just wanted to prove to you and to your Superiors that we are not warped and that we are capable of sustained thought processes and what-have-you. Remember, we have to be on Sunday, August, 16, because Brian and I are leaving/returning to school up North. C'mon guys: let us rock!

respectfully,

Brad and Brian Knapp

P.S Long live Ida Lupino!

There goes the last DJ

Well some folks say they're gonna hang him so high

'Cause you just can't do what he did

There are some things you just can't put in the minds of those kids

As we celebrate mediocrity all the boys upstairs want to see

How much you'll pay for what you used to get for free ....

— Tom Petty, "The Last DJ"

PART FIVE

The Last DJ

Even though the Ida Lupino Liberation Organization did seize control of central Florida's preeminent rock station, Thing One and Thing Two never got on the air as guest DJs.

And that sucked. We were pretty bummed.

If you weren't a musician, you could, by assuming the DJ role, channel the transformational energy of rock music to thousands of loyal local listeners and bask in the glow of their excitement. My brother and I had thought of the guest DJ gig as both a public service—an outreach to our fellow True Believers—and as a quasi-religious experience—acting as mediums in direct communication with the musical divine of that time.

But it didn't happen for us.

At least in the context of rock music's characteristically edgy, rule-breaking, high-energy behavior, the ILLO had acted appropriately. We met Mick Dolan's challenge for wild and crazy Amateur Hour contestants—and exceeded it. To generously paraphrase the angry words of then-program director Bob Church: We had taken things a tad too far.

WDIZ would thrive for a little more than a decade after the ILLO raid. In 1996, the station was struck by another takeover of a far more sinister kind—and never recovered. Hundreds of other rock stations across the country fell victim to the same culprit: the 1996 Telecommunications Act.

In theory, the 1996 Telecommunications Act was implemented to take advantage of new direct-access communication technologies, decrease regulations, reduce consumer costs, and encourage competition. In practice, it achieved only the first two goals. The stark reality was that it unleashed a juggernaut of media consolidation that destroyed locally owned and operated radio stations, crushed the independence and creativity of the few that survived, and decimated the ranks of DJs and station support staff through downsizing and automation.

For the True Believers, it was like living in a sci-fi disaster flick. One day we were grooving to jams and enjoying our favorite DJs as we worked or played. The next day, strange voices started shouting at us nonstop from our speakers. Talk radio reigned supreme, and round-the-clock windbags fanned the flames of credulity, intolerance, and greed. Then the same songs played over and over, at exactly the same times, every day, all week. And when we weren't being brainwashed by bullies, or bored to tears by repetitive programming, we were pestered mercilessly by fast-talking fools trying to sell us stuff.

Oh, my yes. Because the relationship between radio stations and their listeners had changed for the worse. 99% of the stations existed solely as local vendors for 1% of the remote owners and operators who didn't care about the bands or The Music.

Strike that last part.

The remote operators and owners *did* have strong feelings about rock music.

They hated it.

Because rock music was too unpredictable, too individualistic, too inefficient. It didn't make enough money for the station owners. The purpose of the radio station was no longer to showcase the music, to inspire musicians, to incite their fans, or to revel in the excesses of youth, music, and freedom. The sole purpose of the radio station was to sell products. Period. End of story.

In 1996, WDIZ was sold to Paxson Communications, and then flipped to Clear Channel the following year. Clear Channel would become a monster monopoly—the very hydra-headed beast the Telecommunications Act was supposed to kill—with more than 1,200 stations nationwide. The beast's arrival signaled that the end times for indie radio stations had come.

Strangely enough, as the result of the merger mania, we have all become our own DJs, playing tunes on our private amateur hours. But it doesn't feel right to me.

We have Sirius XM, YouTube, podcasts, iMusic, Spotify. We share, we like, we download. With the illusion of our increased personal control comes on-demand depersonalization. There is no room, no time, and no need for spontaneous acts of public enthusiasm. They have been replaced by social media algorithms and downloadable apps. The True Believers devolved from frenzied fans to merely a target audience, monthly subscribers, end users, and other market niches and labels. Unavoidable, perhaps. But we had wanted to be so much more.

The paradox of the WDIZ takeover still haunts me, obviously. We had succeeded for all the wrong reasons: We had resorted to intimidation and implied threat of danger. And yet we had failed for all the right reasons: No self-respecting radio station should reward someone for undermining their authority. My brother and I accepted that paradox for its teachable moment and then moved on—as young adults must—to face all the other paradoxes and illogic required for our maturity, if not necessarily for our happiness.

WDIZ Rock 100 is no longer on the air. Bob Church is dead. So, too, are WDIZ luminaries Mark Samansky and Mike Lyons. Mick Dolan is still kicking, still promoting the station's glory days on Facebook and on the website wdizrock100.com.

And the ILLO? Thing One, Thing Two, Charlie the Tuna, The Rock, The Ace are still around. Their true identities you already know—that is, if you have been reading this five-part series carefully. Their assumed workaday personas are not nearly as interesting, or, sadly, not as much fun. Navigating the midlife river of regrets, the former members of ILLO have a few. But taking over WDIZ the way we did in 1981 is not one of them.

But not torching The Ace's Fire Arrow as the tape deck played Judas Priest's "Burning Up?" Now *that* was a sorely-missed opportunity.

Maybe this will be the year for that?

Thing One and Thing Two

Other Essays

Dreams I'm Never Gonna See

The Winter Stranger

The old 1940s farmhouse was noisy even when everything around it was quiet. Things inexplicably thumped and banged and fell off shelves. Late in the evenings or in the dead of night, empty chairs would groan and squeak. Footsteps sounded frequently on the hardwood floors, but never did we see the feet responsible for the trespass.

Rational yet ill-fitting explanations were explored in defense of the "charm" and "character" that such dilapidated rental houses with acreage hold for young broke impressionable people like myself and my wife-to-be.

Like "I'll bet it's the foundation heaving and settling from swings in temperature."

Mice were also blamed and martyred in droves to preserve domestic tranquility. All solutions were temporary; all theories merely theoretical.

But mice don't move like people do. Mice can't push over a twelve inch cinder block holding a warped wooden closet door closed.

Most provocatively of all, mice don't say "Help me!" in the toy voice I heard one freezing February night.

And they sure as hell don't wear camel hair coats and 1920s-era hats and two-tone shoes and walk through walls.

It was close to nine or ten on that winter night that was becalmed and beautiful wearing several inches of fresh snow. I was seated at a garage sale shop desk in a large living room furnished only with that desk, a lumpy quilted couch, plank and cinder block bookshelves, a gimpy knotty pine coffee table overflowing with books and magazines, and a Buck wood stove that heated fitfully even with a hairdryer aimed at the coals. The overhead room light was off, but next to the little desk was a tall office-type gooseneck lamp that spilled light in a small pool over the desk and adjacent bookshelves. Linda was reading in the adjoining bedroom that had no door; it was blocked off from the living room by a large wool Mexican blanket hung on a curtain rod. I was working on some book reviews for a local arts and entertainment magazine. This was the late 1980s, and my writing wasn't silent. The only sound in the frigid house was the stop-and-start staccato and periodic "ding" of my manual typewriter.

Until someone said "help me."

My writing reverie was broken. I called out to Linda.

"What did you say?"

"I didn't say anything."

And then with great urgency she cried out:

"TURN ALL THE LIGHTS ON! TURN ALL THE LIGHTS ON!"

This was her ... our ... usual drill for those routine enigmatic night noises and falling objects. Per Linda's Boston Irish Catholic upbringing, ghosts, demons, vampires, Balor, banshees, insidious rodents and Jehovah Witnesses—would all cower and scatter before overwhelming displays of electric lighting. Holy Water supposedly had the same effect, but we didn't have any. So I turned the overhead living room light on, then the bedroom light, and finally walked into the kitchen and pulled the chain to the fluorescent light over the sink.

I went back to writing. Linda eventually resumed reading in the now fully-illuminated bedroom.

I heard the voice again, only slightly louder than before. But it was still more whisper than speech or shout.

"Help me."

"Did you say something?"

"NO! TURN ALL THE LIGHTS ON! TURN ALL THE LIGHTS ON!"

But all the lights were already on.

What the—?

It struck me that because of the recent heavy snowfall, maybe someone had driven off the road outside of the farmhouse, which was the last house on the paved portion of the winding mountain road before it degraded to rutted gravel. Was someone calling for help?

I grabbed a flashlight, stepped into my Lacrosse boots, and threw on my Army surplus winter jacket and went outside to see what I could see. Linda was calling out "What is it? What is it?" as I stepped outside and immediately felt the cold tightening my exposed skin. Then Uther, my Blue Heeler, who was kenneled in the spring house not twenty feet away from the main house, demanded to join in the search for the source of the voice in the night.

Together we sniffed and scanned for intriguing scents, tell-tale tire tracks or errant footprints in the deep snow. There were none. We gave up after thirty minutes or so. Uther returned to the spring house, and I went back inside. After explaining to Linda what I had heard but couldn't see, explain, or understand, I resumed working on my reviews.

Another hour or so passed. Linda had turned off her reading light but left the bedroom ceiling light on. The living room light was still on, as well.

Then the voice was so clear, so outside of my own head, so obviously just a few feet behind me.

The voice sounded both human and yet not-quite-human. The pitch and tone grated on my ears the way the recitation from a parrot or pull-string doll can do.

"HELP ME!"

I whirled around, more startled and annoyed than frightened.

"WHAT DO YOU WANT?"

And that's when the figure appeared.

It moved swiftly in front of me, from my right to my left, maybe a body's length away. It was not tall, but not short, either. I was still seated and the form was taller than my sitting posture. It had a forward lean, like someone walking against a strong wind. Looked for all the world like someone from a silent movie or other bygone era. Camel hair knee-length coat with wide collar; a fawn-colored snug-fitting cloche hat with a shiny lighter-colored broad ribbon and bow circling the low-slung hat that rested below where ears should have been. A dark fringe of hair curled out beneath the hat.

The farmhouse living room walls were covered by cheapo 1970s vintage toffee-colored paneling. The figure's clothing stood apart from the background, in full color all its own. I could see an outline of a face peeking out from under the hat: a putty-colored profile with a prominent nose and receding chin. But the face bore no eyes, no expression, no detailed features to offer an identity, or to suggest the absence of a human one.

I remember being more struck by the uncanny movement of the figure than by its preposterous presence. It seemed to speed through the twenty-some feet of the living room in two seconds, like a competitive runner passing by. Yet the short dark length of legs shifting under the coat moved more slowly than the figure itself. It was that eerie rapid soundless stride that made me look at the floor and notice the shoes. I distinctly recall thinking this was a woman, and just as distinctly remember immediately wondering why she was wearing bowling shoes? Because the shoes were two-tone, with the toe and heel portion a light reddish gold, almost blending in with the tongue and groove oak flooring upon which they were noiselessly treading. But the middle of the shoe was darker with visible stitching. Later I realized that the shoes had a true heel, which would have been a definite no-no for bowling shoes. Only much much later was I schooled about the presence of saddle shoes in 1920s fashions, if that was actually what those garments represented.

She sped by me and headed straight for the bedroom wall to my left as I watched her. Not toward the blanketed doorway—toward the wall. And after she passed straight through the bedroom wall, there was a second or two pause until Uther, outside in the spring house, erupted in that outraged bellow all dogs reserve for bears and other formidable intruders, the skin-pebbling howl and antagonistic barking that vocalizes "HEY HEY HEY! WHOOOO THE HELL ARE YOU? HUH? HUH? HUH?"

The figure never showed up again. The strange noises and animated inanimate objects ceased.

My ghost experience didn't seem life-changing to me at the time, or even portentous. Twenty years later, my aging mother would suffer from fear-based delusions so much less real, but so much more vexing than any ghost I could ever imagine. In time, I would connect my wife's reaction to that improbable winter stranger and to her mother-in-law's dementia with her own growing fear-bound universe, which would eventually both include and exclude me.

I'm not sure what to think about ghosts. I guess like my Uther dog, I think they deserve to be noticed and questioned all the same, your own fears be damned.

Dreams I'm Never Gonna See

Isaiah 11:6

*The wolf also shall dwell with the lamb, and the leopard shall lie down
with the kid; and the calf and the young lion and the fatling together;
and a little child shall lead them.*

Isaiah 11:6

A phone message invited me—no, begged me—to shear the loneliest
sheep in all of Red Hill, North Carolina.

*Hel-LO. This is Addie McIntosh, of Red Hill. I don't know if I got the right
number or not. The farm agent gave me this number for the sheep shearing man.
I got just one sheep, she's old, and she needs shearing pretty bad. I used to do it
myself, but can't no more. If you got the time or just coming through this-a-way,
I wished you'd shear this poor sheep for me.*

A second phone message gave me the address and described her
residence. Instantly I knew where it was. I must have driven past the
McIntosh residence a hundred times over the years on my various travels
up and down the mountains and along the snaky curves of NC 226. Her
home was an unremarkable small red brick rancher with attached garage.
Sometimes a big blue Kenworth semi truck was parked in front of it. But
what grabbed my attention was the large solitary sheep standing tethered
to a ramshackle outbuilding and the peculiar structure wrapped in blue
plastic tarps that was situated just behind and to the left of the house.

As a professional sheep shearer and shepherd, I would study the sheep
and ponder its destiny. Why was it being kept in one spot and not allowed
to graze further? How long had it been keeping its lonely vigil there?
How did it avoid being savaged by dogs or coyotes while neck-tied to the
outbuilding that had no surrounding perimeter fencing? Did someone put
it up overnight in the outbuilding that had only one busted window and
one warped door? Had it ever been properly shorn?

The sheep looked large-framed and rounded out enough in the haunch to suggest it was getting enough to eat. But my passing appraisal made from distance of over 200 feet and at 35 mph— couldn't be a reliable one. A sheep can look okay from a distance but actually be rotting underneath all that wool.

But an even bigger mystery nagged at me. What was lurking behind the blue tarps? I had to know. Just the way I'm built. If I took the job, I would find out.

In my life, all the best gigs didn't pay. There are the things I did for the money—and then there are the things I did for the mystery and the memory. And the two never seemed to meet up. Sheep shearing was definitely in the latter category.

When I finally returned her phone calls, Addie confirmed that she could satisfy the basic needs of an itinerant sheep shearer who used mechanical shearing equipment. She could keep the sheep in the dry and off feed the day before I arrived. She had a level spot of ground roughly the size of the shearer's sheet of plywood. The makeshift shearing stand had electric power close by. I didn't press her too hard for details. It was only one old sheep, anyway.

So early one dewy May morning, I pulled my little truck into the McIntosh driveway, scanned the intriguing blue tarps for clues, and then walked toward the house.

Coming out the front door to meet me was the slightly bent form of Addie McIntosh. She was one of those genuine mountain folks who looked anywhere from fifty to five hundred years old, depending on what was going on that day. She balled her iron gray hair into a thick bun and wore an oversized red plaid hunting jacket over a long denim skirt. The skin on her face was sallow, textured like crepe paper. She was wreathed in cigarette smoke. Her hands were big for her small frame, reddened by weather, swollen from work, but still strong-looking and scaly with callus. I shook one of them in greeting and I asked her straight off.

"Tell me Miz McIntosh—what's in that big box-like thing there with the blue tarps on it?"

"A woof." She took a deep drag off her cigarette, and nodded to herself. "Yep."

I paused way too long. "You say a woof?"

"Mmm hmm. A woof. Craziest ole thing you'd ever want to see." She frowned and crossed her arms and shook her head in disagreement with the thought of it. "I'd like to have throwed a blue duck fit when my son brung him home. He got him from somewheres way up north. Some feller just gave it to him and he brought it down in his truck." She took the last draw on the nib of her cigarette and coughed out that she had no use for the blamed thing.

Addie told me how her son had got saved a few years back. He went away who knows where and came back with a wolf. She pronounced it "woof," which sounded better to me than the usual way. Anyway, her son wanted the wolf and a sheep to live together, like it says in the Bible. So her son got the wolf, and then he bought this old sheep to go with it. Addie went on to tell me her son was a trucker and how he was gone much of the time. She had to feed the wolf and clean up after it. The sheep she didn't mind, as she had been raised up with them. But the wolf aggravated her something terrible. She said she was going broke feeding the wolf hamburger all the time, like her son told her to do. She worried that it would escape somehow and kill somebody's livestock or pet. Or get shot, or get run-over by a car. Then her son would be upset with her. Now her health had gone poorly lately, and the old sheep was too big for her to shear anymore.

I asked Addie "when did you last shear her?"

"Two years ago."

"What did you shear her with?"

"Pair of scissors."

"Do you mean the old-timey sheep shearing blades that look kinda like small hedge trimmers?"

"No, I mean scissors. Like the kind I have in my sewing box."

"Take you long to do it?"

"Law, mercy, yes! About most of a day. I was plum wore out, after. Can I get you a cup of coffee before you start?"

"No m'am, thank you, anyway. But before I start, can I take a look at your wolf?"

"He's not my woof, but go ahead."

I had to see the wolf. I was trying not to think about my impending difficulties with shearing an old sheep covered in matted dreadlocks of overgrown wool.

I slowly walked around the covered front of the kennel's chain-link fencing and looked.

And there it was.

At first the wolf was lying down at the far end of the kennel, just a long black and gray shadow on the greenish-gray concrete slab. The long head was aimed towards me, the thick tail curled around its body. It panted lightly, exhaling puffs of silvery mist in the cool moist mountain air. Its ears flicked now and then at unseen flies and gnats trespassing upon them. The black nose pulsed, working me over at a distance. Then, as if sparked by some kind of recognition or just a laundry list of questions about me, the wolf perked up and unfolded long legs and stood on huge feet. As it began to pace silently back and forth, ears pricking, the head bobbing with interest, I could see that it was a male. I watched his long limbs dance silently inside the kennel. His enormous paws traipsed gingerly across the concrete pad, making only the slightest contact with its surface, as if it were red hot. His rough coat of charcoal and ash turned into a smoky fringe around his neck, framing the keen face and glowing agates for eyes.

Man and wolf regarded each other. He stared at me, through me, in me, for me. His intense scrutiny was equal parts challenge and invitation.

As he padded to and fro, studying me, I felt the grip of connection between us, like the feeling of previous acquaintance. He cast the conflicting impressions of being either an enormous beast with a very light presence, or a smallish creature with an overpowering one. One couldn't be sure which—and that is the unnerving difference between wolves and dogs. I couldn't swear to it, but I thought I saw him wink at me and stretch the black rubbery borders of his mouth into a grin.

I left the wolf and trudged out to the little shed with Addie to assess the sheep and the shearing chore before me.

The old ewe was standing forlornly inside the shed, with her head poking through the glassless window frame. As we approached her, she called out a few times, as if to confirm that Addie had been able to keep her off feed long enough for her to be hungry. Which was a good start, anyway. A sheep with a full belly was always difficult and messy to shear. You could kill an old sheep by shearing them in that condition. The pressure on their heart and lungs would be too much.

As I looked at the sheep through the broken window, my misgivings about the day ahead were confirmed. She was large-framed but gaunt, with her hipbones making prominent points underneath the tufts of wool. Her coarse gray-brown fleece was impregnated with dirt and debris. Great billowing swaths of felted wool ringed her neck and hung from her flanks. The weight of the clotted fleece would pull on the ewe's aging thin skin, almost certainly inviting shearing cuts.

I patted her down for the usual concealed weapons carried by unshorn sheep. Thick thorns, twigs, weed stalks. Pine cones. Nails and fence staples. Strands of barbed wire or hay baling twine. Things that would shred my fingers as they plunged blindly into the heavy fleece. Or worse, get lodged between the comb and the furious blur of the moving cutters and lock up the shearing handpiece, causing it to jump from my hand and become a deadly missile. I had to dig deep to find the frayed plastic dog collar buried beneath the fierce tangles covering her skinny old neck. Her fleece had the raspy unyielding texture and consistency of a doormat. It took me longer to unbuckle the collar and pull it free than it would to have half-sheared another sheep in better condition. Not such a good start.

The sheep gazed at me dully, her golden eyes expressionless. I rubbed the frizzy flannel between her ears. She hung her bony head, resigned to whatever fate awaited her. I spoke to her, trying to sound hopeful, more for my own sake than for Addie or the sheep.

"Well, old girl, we're gonna give you a new 'do, make you all pretty. What do you think of that?"

She moaned out a single *baah* in reply. Her breath was pungent, like sour milk and old lawn clippings souped together and overheating on a stove.

It would not be her last word on the subject.

It took two trips between the shed and my truck to retrieve my equipment. My shearer's sheet of plywood was on the ground, my little military surplus bag of first aid supplies for both sheep and man hung from nail angling out of the doorway, my tackle box of combs, cutters, and other tools sat close at hand. Since there was only one sheep to shear, I didn't bother setting up my shearing machine. Instead, I chose my trusty old Oster Shearmaster electric clippers. The Shearmaster operated just like any barber's clippers, only louder and more unwieldy. At over a foot long and weighing five pounds, the Shearmaster tended to heat up quickly and make a high-pitched snarl that no mammal, two-legged or four, could tolerate for long. To the uninitiated, it was like using a psychotic chihuahua with a spiking fever to chew the hairs off another animal. But it was usually up to the task of grooming a sheep or two. All you had to do was plug it in and go to town.

So that's what I did. I fitted a wide-toothed comb that would help get through the unwelcome mat the old sheep's fleece had become. I placed the 4-point cutter on the comb bed and adjusted the tension between the two, oiled the cutting surfaces, and plugged the long clipper cord into the old-timey porcelain light bulb socket with an electric outlet built into the side.

And the clipper cord fell out of the socket. Repeatedly. Maddeningly.

No matter how I bent the plug prongs or prayed silently for the outlet to hang onto them, the cord dropped and the Shearmaster died. A couple of times the plug held just long enough for me to grab up the sheep and sit her down on her butt, straddle her back and shoulders, and just begin my first shearing stroke high up on her rib cage—and then nothing.

I would ask Addie to plug me back in. There would be a few seconds of angry humming promise, then abrupt silence. Addie offered to hold the cord in place, and she did that for awhile. But the outlet had a short somewhere, and the current would not flow reliably. The sight of Addie's stringy arm outstretched, shaking with the strain of holding the clipper cord into that cursed outlet, struck me as some kind of sad mockery of the Statue of Liberty. Give me your tired, poor old sheep, a huddled mass of wool, yearning to be cut free.

But it wasn't happening.

The sheep sat patiently through the frustration, panting slightly but making no protest about her prolonged sitting on a wooden board and being cradled between a man's legs.

"Miz McIntosh, I'm sorry, but I don't think this is working too well."

"No, it's not. That's a fact."

Addie frowned as she fumbled into the pocket of her jacket for her cigarettes and lighter.

After a few puffs of contemplation, she came up with the notion of bringing the old sheep closer to the house. The garage itself was a mess, she allowed, full of her son's junk. But there was a flat area over yonder, close to the rear of the house, and an outlet in the covered garage. An extension cord would connect the power to my clippers, and I would be shearing in the shade of a big maple. Wouldn't it be a shame to come all the way out this way and not shear this poor old sheep?

I prodded her poor old sheep to its feet and held onto her as Addie described the alternative shearing arrangement.

"Are you talking about that spot over there ... right next to where the wolf is?"

"Yep. It won't bother him none at all. All he cares about is his ole hamburg' meat."

All I cared about was finishing the job. Addie wanted the same. The sheep baahed a few times and tried to return to the comfort of her familiar patch of grass, but I held her back.

I didn't like the proposed setup. No shearer wants to shear a sheep in an unconfined area, let alone right next to a barely-contained wolf.

I figured the old sheep wasn't a real flight risk. Even if she did manage to wiggle free from me, she likely wouldn't go far. Probably stop a few yards away and start cropping the lush lawn in the backyard.

But what would the wolf do when the air filled with the chatter of clippers and the tantalizing aroma of fresh lanolin and more mutton than he could eat in a day?

I pictured the predator ripping aside the woven fencing and savaging us both, maybe even Addie for good measure. I had heard horror stories of livestock guardian breeds, huge Anatolian Shepherds and Great Pyrenees, getting so worked up by the raucous wrestling match between man and sheep that they became unmanageable. Even herding dogs like Border Collies had been known to leap into the fray, with disastrous consequences.

The sheep called out and stamped a hoof, as if to say "just get this over with it so I can eat." There was nothing to do but finish the job.

I threaded the collar back through the wool and around the sheep's neck and reattached the rope tie. Addie stood with the sheep and petted her while I carried all of my gear over to the back of the house and placed it next to the wolf kennel. The wolf was lying down at the far end of the kennel, ears at half-mast, looking upon my labors with mild interest.

I tested the new outlet. It worked. I checked to see how the wolf reacted to the noise of the clippers. His ears stiffened and swiveled fully forward toward the sound. His nose was working something out, probably the smell of the clipper's lubricating oil. But the rest of him appeared unmoved and remained unmoving. Things were looking up again.

I walked back over to Addie and the sheep and removed the collar again. I stuck my thumb inside the sheep's mouth, right in the gap between the front grass-cutting teeth and the rear grinding teeth. Making a ring with the thumb and middle finger of my left hand, and grabbing the knobby stump of the sheep's docked tail with my right, I pushed, pulled, and prodded the sheep the hundred feet or so to the new shearing spot under the majestic shade of a sugar maple. Addie followed close behind, occasionally exhorting the slow-moving animal to get a move on.

With the clippers lying on the plywood and right next to my foot, I hugged the sheep from the side of its body and then turned her head toward her outside shoulder. At the same time, I pushed down on her outside hip. As she collapsed onto the board, I quickly spun her onto her butt with her legs facing out in front of her. I grabbed up the clippers and with a flick of a dial they screamed out for wool. I made a final short pivot to make sure the clipper cord trailed behind me and not in the way of the shearing strokes I would soon make.

As I turned slightly, flipping the cord over my shoulder, the sheep's lolling head and my own suddenly faced the wolf. He was now standing next to the fence, less than six feet away from the sheep's outstretched rear hooves.

Wolf and sheep regarded each other.

The ancient forlorn sheep changed instantly, changed utterly. She did a double-take—or as much as a sheep can be said to do one. But it was no trick of anthropomorphism to realize that the sheep had seized up with alarm. She had recognized her eternal enemy, either by clearer sight or closer smell. It didn't matter which. Fight or flight was coming. Maybe both.

The sheep glared at the wolf. The wolf stood motionless and returned her stare.

I could feel the sheep's body swell with purpose, like a garden hose filling with water. The legs curled inward, each growing taut as a drawn bow. Suddenly she bolted like a bucking bronco, her front legs galloping wildly in the air, her rear legs exploding outward and down, drumming on the plywood with her frantic attempt for traction and escape. I leaned down to press her closer to my legs and to keep her from getting to at least two of her feet. She responded with two front leg jabs to my face. One of her snaggle-sharp hooves found my eye socket,

BAAAH!

"Ahhh!"

I probed for blood or eyeball jelly escaping me. None detected. The sheep began pistoning her limbs and rocking her body so violently that I could barely hold her between the cradle of my legs. Just as she was about to jerk to one side and gain her footing, I held onto her neck and tried to control her wildly-waving head with my thumb-in-the-mouth trick. She countered by ducking her head with great force and speed, dislodging my thumb from the safety of the tooth gap. My thumb dislocated backwards and crunched between her molars. A sickening jet of pain shot up my left arm.

The sheep had drawn first blood.

I gathered the combative creature back into a semblance of the position required for the first few shearing strokes down her belly and along the inside of her thighs. I buried my throbbing and bleeding left thumb under her fleece and next to her skin, hoping the sheep grease would at least staunch the flow so neither of us would look like extras in a slasher film.

Sweat began to rain down from my face and burn its way into the corners of my eyes as I hung desperately to the struggling sheep. Even as her offending coat fell away from her stroke by stroke, and cooling breezes caressed her skin for the first time in years—she fought on. Worse, as I progressed down her flanks and sheared the inside of her thighs and lower legs, she redoubled her efforts to maim me. Her back legs lashed out with such lightning speed that even a karate master would have been envious. The frantic limbs would scissor and snag the power cord, winding it up like spaghetti on a fork. This resulted in the Shearmaster being snatched this way and that, either unplugging itself or sending the sharp comb and cutting teeth hurtling toward her or me with equal menace. When kicks and jabs didn't work, the furious beast borrowed some hidden power from somewhere in the cosmos, the way sci-fi movie monsters did when things went south. With her new-found strength she jacknifed her entire body like some mutant furry shrimp and scooted her way again and again off the plywood. Each time I would have to haul her back to the center of the board.

I viewed with grim satisfaction the dark clouds of dirty wool falling away from the pinkish body, leaving corduroy rows of light golden fuzz and occasional cotton candy tufts of wool clinging protectively over her protruding bones. Slowly but surely, this sheep was being shorn.

About thirty minutes had passed—the time it would normally take me to do ten sheep—and I was only half finished. I was exhausted. I was in pain. I was about to say something self-pitying to Addie when I felt summoned somehow, for some reason, to eye the wolf.

I could see him standing there like a statue. His previous thousand-yard stare had changed to the look of a disappointed sports fan whose favorite team was losing the game.

The wolf invaded my consciousness with his own. My focus on the shearing strokes was obliterated.

Was I hallucinating? Had fatigue and frustration robbed me of my faculties? Did the sheep scramble my brains with one of its left hooks?

Surreal scenarios played out before my mind's eye. The wolf and I were walking together through 10,000 years of interwoven purpose. The two of us were mutually transforming. We were evolving in sync. The old 60's hit by The Turtles—"So Happy Together"—had begun to play somewhere in my head. The resulting reverie established itself in a series of incongruous past life regressions. Their timing was terrible, given that an old but no longer frail sheep was in the process of kicking the shit out of me.

First, I was striding across endless primeval grassland. With spear and knife and dressed in animal hides, I strode confidently as the wolf loped toward me, a meal for two dangling from its bloody maw .....

Then, we were making our way through a bustling frontier town in the Old West, dodging carriages, mule-drawn wagons and riders on horses. The utility of my wolf companion was manifest. There he was, scattering bothersome mongrels, children and good-for-nothings with a hint of a growl and bared teeth .....

Finally, we were playing games in a modern city park, the wolf now refined—some would say reduced—to a playful dog. Acrobatic and tireless, he plucked the soaring Frisbee out of the muggy summer air while overweight middle-aged men lashed to tiny attitudinous pets looked on with and envy and regret … .

BWA-AAAAAAAAAAGH!

The sheep cared little about my reveries. She was enraged by my assault on her unkempt solitude. She was appalled by my betrayal.

Yes, betrayal. To her, I had breached and breached egregiously, the domestication agreement my people had made with her kind more than six millennia ago. We had promised to 1) lead her into green pastures; 2) protect her against wolves; 3) never ever use a whirring chirping buzzing burning metal shearing machine anywhere near her, so help us that pastoral, sheep-loving God. Amen.

She was painfully reminding me that *we* had evolved together, too. Centuries of inbreeding had made her incapable of shedding her wool. She was forced to have this annual brawl with brutes like me who showed little common sense but possessed strong backs and sharp haircutting instruments.

BAWWWWWWWW!

But as the volume of her outrage increased, and the more violent her exertions did become—the wolf, in poignant contrast, grew calm, diminished in its capacity for mayhem. His quietude was engaging, like that of a meditating yogi.

The twisted calculus of my dilemma was this: The sheep equaled danger, the wolf, benevolence.

In the time it took for the kick of a sheep's leg, the wolf had morphed into the picture of Nipper, the famous RCA dog listening to "His Master's Voice" coming from a gramophone. The wolf's long smiling head was cocked quizzically towards us. His penetrating eyes widened slightly with each new sheep scream.

He sat perfectly still. The only movement from him was his tongue flicking at his lips and nose.

In the worst of situations, a quiet rational voice seems to persist somehow, somewhere, if only in one's panicked imagination. In this instance, it seemed to come from the wolf. His calm counsel wafted over from his direction, deftly penetrating the buzz of the shearing machine, the drum beat of sheep hooves striking human flesh and bone, the sheep bellowing, the man cussing.

Regardless of the implausibility of its source, the message could not be ignored. The wolf knew me by name.

"Trust your feelings, Brian Lee. Use force."

BAWWWWWWW!

"That sheep is making life difficult for you both. If you'd let me out of this cage, I **know** I could help you with your unfortunate situation there ... ."

BA-AAAAAAAAGH!

The wolf had become Socrates with a tail. He was Obi-Wan Kenobi with fangs and fur.

I was becoming desperate from the struggle and nearly blind from my own stinging sweat and filth kicked up by the unhinged sheep. I tried to ignore The Reasonable Voice and chastised myself back to attentiveness with the thought of the Bible verse in Luke 15, the parable of the lost sheep. But I could only come up with a blasphemous sheep shearer's version: "What man, having sheared a hundred sheep, when he has to shear only One of them, doth forget the ninety and nine already shorn, and still go after that One which is a total Psycho Loser from Hell?"

And then ... it was done. A skinny pinkish-white nappy-looking Dr. Seuss-like character lay panting on the plywood. Blood was smeared in stripes across her fuzzy hide. But she had no cuts. That blood was mine. The piles of wool scattered on the board's edges and into the yard could have filled the bed of a pickup truck. That poor old sheep needed to be shorn for sure.

Even Addie cracked a tight smile of approval.

"She looks kinda funny, though, don't she? I bet she feels better having all that hot wool off her. Know I would."

Before I walked the sheep back to her shed, I took a minute to get a second wind and watch the wolf for clues. But the wolf, having spoken his inner thoughts to me, said nothing further. Though I never saw him move, he must have retreated to the far end of the kennel just as I had finished the last shearing pass on the far left side of the sheep's rump. His manner returned to the stoic lupine captive of Biblical imagination.

My left thumb has never worked right since. Mystery and memory be damned.

The Potato Patch

Amazing how a twenty- by fifty-foot strip of hard clay soil, cut off by a bold creek on one end and a dead-end road on the other, could mean so much.

I live on a small farm that's steep as a mule's face and configured like a derby hat that's had the back half cut away. The only available flat land lies like the hat's narrow brim, curving along the contour of the aforementioned bold creek that divides my property from my neighbor's. Our house clings to the looming wooded hillside like a buckle on the hatband. When my wife and I bought our place in Yancey County back in the 80s, the only existing rights-of-way were a walk bridge thirty feet long and a bushel-basket wide, and an oak-planked drive bridge that lay at the bottom of an abrupt hill some three hundred feet from the house.

My neighbor had this nice level strip of land that led to what could be a natural driveway of bottomland along our side of the creek and right up to our house. The strip had potatoes planted, but nothing else. Tangles of catbrier and blackberry cane coiled along the sides. Bee balm and stinging nettle settled thickly near the border with the creek.

The potato patch appeared to profit him little. But it promised us a safer, more efficient way to bring firewood closer to the home that would burn it for winter warmth.

Everybody called my neighbor "Sonny," even though he was in his 60s by then. A tall man, all nose, sinews, and cigarettes, Sonny didn't suffer fools or beggars. Or flatlanders who might turn out to be both.

We waited two years before asking.

"Sonny, do you think you might want to sell that little potato patch to us so we can throw a bridge across it?"

His craggy face darkened and his mouth folded into layers of resistance.

"Naw, I don't think I would."

We let the matter be.

A few years later, the matter resurrected itself. I had rebuilt the walk bridge, but only wide enough for three men and a boy to carry a woodstove across it, which happened twice. I had almost driven my truck off the icy plank bridge several winters in a row, too. I'll not detail our yearly ordeal of using mules to drag down—and humans to hand carry—firewood logs to the house, except to point out that "death by mule" is excluded by many a homeowner's insurance policy.

It was too much aggravation. It would be simpler to buy split firewood and truck it over that flat potato patch and haul the wood right up to the house.

I dearly desired that potato patch.

One summer, I saw Sonny sneaking toward the roadside corner of the potato patch. He had hornet spray in one hand, a small gas can in the other. I noticed raised red blotches on his leathery arms and one centered on his forehead.

"Lo, there, Sonny. What are you into?"

"Lo, Brian. Got a big yellerjackets' nest there. Them sorry boogers deviled me for the last time. I got somethin' right here they'll remember me by!"

I watched him spray the hole, splash it with gas, then toss his cigarette on it. There was a huff of ignition, a ball of flame that rolled away and blended with the summer's heat, followed by a few stray wisps of smoke that arced toward the ground, wiggled a bit, then curled up dead.

I shared his satisfaction. Then I asked him about the potato patch.

"You ever sell your potatoes?"

"Naw. Wouldn't make nothin' if I did. The big stores sell them ones from Ida-ho so cheap it's un-real."

"You just grow them for yourself?"

"Yep. A man won't starve so long as he's got taters dug in somewheres."

"Well, if a man was to pay you three times the value of all the potatoes you could ever dig up in a year—just so he could get at his firewood—would you take it?"

He frowned and spat.

"Loggin' would compact the soil. Hit would be ruined."

I fought back.

"But no more than your tractor's wheels do every year?"

"I think it would. Nosir, I wouldn't allow it."

The score: Sonny 2, Me 0.

Years later, Sonny trapped a 'coon down there. He was 80 by then. He was scared to dispose of it because he was sure it was rabid, which he pronounced "ray-bid." I got rid of it for him. He was grateful. He got talkative and lapsed into telling hunting tales.

I sensed another opportunity. It was now or never.

In my dreams, I would gamble everything, promise anything. I'd smother him with truckloads of organic potatoes, pave the patch's borders with hand-painted tiles bearing the likenesses of Sonny and Dale Earnhardt, enrich the soil with the finest manure from champion show cattle.

But face to face with the man, I could only offer this.

"Sonny, I'd like to buy that potato patch from you. Name your cash price, and I'll gladly pay it."

He was silent for too long. His face gave away nothing.

When he finally spoke, he looked at his feet as it came out softly, steadily—history aimed at the ground.

"Papaw John grew his taters here. Taters had always been grown here. 'Backer and corn everywhere else, but taters from right here."

And then his final word on the matter.

"You just want this piece of land. You don't need it. But I do. And I'll not sell it for love nor money."

He'd made his point. I won't ask him again.

You got to keep straight what you want from what you need.

Dreams I'm Never Gonna See

The Greatest Little Hero

On the seventh day of August in 1974, at the tender but rapidly over-cooking age of thirteen, I finally found a hero who made sense to me.

Warner Brothers cartoons still guided me spiritually through the obstacle course of puberty—and would continue to guide me for the next three decades. But Bugs Bunny was a Trickster Hero whose celluloid realm excluded the laws of physics that were becoming painfully unavoidable by thirteen. He could inspire but not lead; he deserved worship but not emulation.

I was abandoning the world of Marvel comics because, frankly, who was I trying to kid? My few attempts at flight had landed me in the ER. X-ray vision would actually be horrifying. My adamantine claws were not forming but my *horns* were, so to speak, for girls. And no one gets laid in the world of Marvel, alas.

The world of men? J. Gordon Liddy, the so-called superpatriot who roasted his hand over a flame to prove his loyalty to a fascist paranoid already on the ropes of impeachment that summer (Nixon would resign the following day)? No thank you.

Muhammad Ali? A beautiful, brave, defiant hero, without a doubt. But he had lost to Frazier, and Norton had broken his jaw, and by August 1974, he had yet to stun the world with his victory over Foreman. He was The Greatest, someone to watch in awe, but still not quite The One for me.

There were others, but their facts and feats would require sorting for years.

At thirteen, you don't wait for things. And that included heroes.

But in the summer of '74, while cruising the 'hood in my low-slung, chopper-forked Stingray, desperate for action and inspiration in equal measure, accompanied by the hazy heat of a Midwestern summer and the glorious soundtrack provided by radios tuned to WLS – Chicago wherever I went—I didn't have to wait.

Because The Hero appeared.

And he appeared in the most improbable guise imaginable. A little red-haired Frenchman with a sissy name like Philippe Petit.

But oh, what that short, sissy-named Frenchman did.

Early that morning on the seventh day of August 1974, Petit had walked across a wire suspended between the brand-new World Trade Towers.

It bears repeating.

He walked, for almost an hour, back and forth, by himself, on a cable that was suspended a quarter of a mile above the sizzling New York streets and 140 feet between the Trade Towers.

He did it all perfectly. Illegally. Irresistibly. In spite of all the odds and obstacles. In defiance of all the cops and nay-sayers and rubberneckers and the crosswinds and the shimmying cable and the swaying twin monsters of reinforced concrete and steel that simultaneously held his fate yet promised him immortality, too.

It would later be called "the artistic crime of the century." Documentaries would be made and imitators would appear. But I knew it for what it was, right then and there. I didn't have to wait for adults and the media talking heads (then mercifully less prevalent) to explain away what intuitively I felt in my heart and knew in my head even at the slightly-crazed age of thirteen.

Philippe Petit gave the most important life lesson a true hero can impart: the shortest distance between two impossible points is always yourself.

Thank you, Philippe Petit. *Tu m'as sauvé la vie!*

The Art of Thomas Kinkade

Thomas Kinkade is reportedly the most collected living artist in the world. A list of all the Kinkade collections, gallery catalogs, co-authored religious inspiration books, home décor spin-offs, architectural plans, etc., ad nauseum, would match the size and content of the Asheville phone directory.

As the work of an avowed Christian, Kinkade's art has been described as being dedicated to evoking an overwhelming longing for the peace, tranquility, and light-drenched orderliness of our pre-lapsarian existence. That his artistic and moral vision has inspired exclusive planned communities and pricey golf resorts seems to be an incidental—although to Kinkade, certainly not an undesirable—achievement.

Indeed, Kinkade-inspired galleries, limited-edition prints, and gift shop-related knockoffs constitute no mere cottage industry, although he does demonstrate a marked obsession for painting quaint Tudor-style cottages.

It is the pervasive acceptance of and clamor for the materialistic manifestations of Kinkade's rather limited artistic vision—the sanctification, if you will, of his penchant for depopulated and nonsensical rural scenery—that serves to only increase the hair-lifting horror that lurks beneath his sun-dappled streams and glowing rustic manses.

Yes, horror. Horror of the worst kind, the horror wrought from juxtaposing innocuous items or idyllic surroundings with sudden ghastly consequences. The kind of thought-erasing horror that comes from watching a huge cylindrical brush used in an automatic car wash smash through your windshield. The kind of throat-parching, temple-pounding, sweaty-knees horror that comes from watching the stitched simpleton's smile on a Raggedy Ann doll suddenly gape open into a bloody drooling leer.

Do not misunderstand me, here. Kinkade's art does not evoke Clown Fear, or Marionette Fear, or Dick Cheney Fear, or Disney Audio-Animatronic Fear—I'm talking about that Mother of All Fears: *When Paradise Turns into Hell.*

For this Halloween, if you want to scare the dickens out of discerning adults and impressionable children, forget about the works of Poe, King, or Koontz.

Just take a *good* look at the artwork of Thomas Kinkade.

Upon close examination, Kinkade's rural dystopias appear to possess the following common themes:

1) Hellish glow seen emanating from every closed window to every sealed-up cottage, clock tower, inn, horse barn, church, etc. *All* of Kinkade's structures seem consumed from within by raging infernos. What might be laughed off as artistic excess suddenly trickles icily down your spine when you realize that Kinkade's rustic incinerators are operating at full tilt regardless of the time of day, the prevailing weather conditions, and the particular season depicted in the painting!

2) All of his structures bear multiple chimneys that are exhaling thin, vertically-stretched spires of exhaust smoke which are indicative of extremely hot fires within, and of virtually no air movement without. Again, these chimneys are operating in all seasons and weather conditions. Why are the fires burning so hotly all the time? What's cooking? *You don't want to know!*

3) There is an inexplicable absence of people, despite the presence of livestock, abandoned agricultural implements, raging chimney fires, what have you. In Kinkade's peaceful landscapes, it seems as if a sort of esthetically-directed neutron bomb had detonated, leaving standing only the charming buildings, bucolic beasts and majestic landscape.

There is something *terrible* going on in these paintings.

Yet millions of consumers seem drawn, moth-like, to Kinkade's infernal little countrified scenes, nevertheless.

Of course, it is tempting to cast Kinkade, a.k.a. "Painter of Light," in a Lucifer-like role (remember, *Lucifer* in Latin means "light bringer"). Yet a more compelling explanation for the incongruous elements in his deceptively warm and fuzzy-feeling art is that Kinkade has placed them there deliberately, and that it is not Kinkade's evil that so many people are attracted to, but rather their own.

That is to say, then, that Thomas Kinkade's art might be completely misunderstood, and that the sheer audacity and brilliance of his cunningly-wrought moral didacticism has been completely ignored.

Kinkade could possibly be our Dante, with limited editions available now on eBay; our Brueghel, hidden in the back of *Southern Living*, experienced only while you are idly flipping through the magazines at the dentist's office.

Like Hieronymus Bosch, Kinkade's religious fervor seems to revel in the hell-bound procession of contemporary sinners. But unlike the 15th century artist, Kinkade does not resort to fantastic monsters or gruesomely apocalyptic scenes to depict their perdition. Rather, Kinkade's genius lies in both his understanding and rendering of contemporary human frailty in terms of the lurid, irresistible appeal of idealized real estate. For Bosch, it was the bubble-bosomed, jewel-laden temptresses and the winged demons with fish eyes and spiked tails swinging mowing-scythes who represented the driving forces behind Renaissance depravity. For Kinkade, the ultimate context for modern evil is the seemingly static, wholly-controlled, wholly-contrived resort environment that attempts to evoke a pre-lapsarian perfection yet with all the amenities: A bed and breakfast Eden where NO OTHER PEOPLE can interfere with one's vacation. Kinkade traps us within our own vanity and illusions, and then begins burning down the quaint little houses. The Puritan preacher Jonathan Edwards would have sinners clenched fast in the hands of an angry god. Kinkade would have them locked inside thatched roof stone cottages, begging pyromaniac realtors and resort managers for mercy that never comes.

And in the comfy painting, the horses graze on, indifferent to the screams hurled against the stone walls and the rosy windows shut fast for eternity. Maybe those aren't even horses in Kinkade's "A Perfect Summer Day"—they're Centaurs! And this time, Virgil the Caretaker isn't around to guide you safely through the pastoral Inferno that Thomas Kinkade, the "master of light," has cleverly created.

Happy Halloween, folks!

Considering Gratitude
and Cat Jeoffry

For I am possessed of a cat, surpassing in beauty, from whom
I take occasion to bless Almighty God ... .

— Christopher Smart, fragment from *Jubilate Agno*

I looked out my back window and saw a heavy snow slanting across my view. The relentless winter had pursued me into April. I took the affront personally.

Then my dogs entered the scene. They both looked up in unison at the whirling flakes, their noses working it all out. Then their mouths opened slightly and their smiles fell out. They looked at each other and immediately began to wrestle and chew, hurling each other about the soggy ground.

They made me smile. I was grateful to them. And gratitude doesn't come easy for me.

I don't mean I have a problem acknowledging my indebtedness to others. On the contrary, I think I have a heightened awareness of that stern and inflexible Inner Accountant who diligently records all *quid pro quo* arrangements and who demands a balanced book.

But I think gratitude is more than repaying debts, returning favors, or, more darkly, evening the score.

Gratitude is an elevated condition of well-being, an ecstatic state of acceptance that is not inert or passive, but vividly alive and dynamic. It's damn hard work to be grateful, because you have to truly perceive, from moment to moment, the value of whatever is given—or taken away—and, within that perception, find joy in accepting that it will all come out to be the same in the end, no matter what.

No matter what.

The Inner Accountant would not agree with this at all.

But listen—I knew of a man who was truly grateful. I think about him from time to time. About him and his cat.

For I will consider my Cat Jeoffy.
For he is the servant of the Living God,
duly and daily serving him.

Christopher "Kit" Smart had been a brilliant scholar at Cambridge, but chucked it all to become a wildly creative Grub Street hack writer. Soon, though, that enterprise also proved too limiting for his manic energies. So he began to stage subversive street performances.

At first, these performances were deemed to lowbrow to be dangerous. And they were hilarious, to boot. Dressed up as "Mary Midnight," an imposing, outspoken old midwife with a high-crowned hat, Smart opened up his shows with a ranting sermon that would have delighted Monty Python fans even today. This was followed by his faithful retinue of dwarves, one-legged dancers, fiddlers, fart-men, learned dogs, slapstick clowns and other provocative entertainers.

Smart's performances faces stiff competition from mid-18th century London's cockfights, dogfights, freak shows, wax works, women gladiators, puppet shows, jugglers, acrobats, et al. And then there were those popular, ever-compelling displays of punishment, indicative of an enlightened and conservative era: Whippings, brandings, cudgelings, breakings-on-the-wheel, hangings, and so on. Nevertheless, Smart's crazy little show was much in demand at the Haymarket, Castle Tavern, and Southwark Fair.

But then he started to do something *weird*.

He dispensed with his players, performing solo all over London.

On his knees.

Worse yet, he badgered his friends, acquaintances, passers-by—everyone he could get his hands on—into performing with him.

For he keeps the Lord's watch in the night
against the adversary.
For he counteracts the powers of darkness
by his electrical skin & glaring eyes.

The public did cut him a little slack at first. They knew he was an excitable little man given to excesses. And the strain of providing for a family, coupled with his literary, theatrical, and social activities, often proved too much for Smart to bear. Samuel Johnson and other *literati* had grown accustomed to seeing him work nonstop for days on his street oratories, only to collapse in the taverns afterwards.

As his solo performances grew more intense and passionate, so, too, did the public's dismay.

The Age of Reason frowned on public displays of emotion, of ecstatic transport, unless they were associated with punishment. Even more disturbing was Smart's sincerity, which was confirmed by his refusal to accept money for his act.

The Inner Accountant was born in the 18th century—and likely the Outer Accountant was, too. And both agreed that practically anything was understandable and acceptable, so long as it could be placed within the context of commerce.

Even gratitude.

The alarming spectacle presented by Christopher Smart was … his kneeling and praying in the streets.

By 1756, Smart's excesses had earned him, in his own words, "a dangerous fit of illness." But upon his recovery, he believed it was the Lord who had delivered him out of it.

And he was just so … *grateful* to be alive and back on the streets of London, amid the beggars and thieves and prostitutes and linkboys and peddlars and footmen and gentry. Surrounded by open sewers and chamber pots and butcher's wastes and turpentine works and syphilitic lechers who would not—could not—change their linen undergarments often enough.

He was delighted with it all.

He saw evidence of God's providential plan everywhere he looked. He wanted to make everyone else see it, too.

He *had* to make everyone see it. It would be the artistic challenge of his life, the most rewarding street theater he could ever imagine.

Jubilate Agno. Rejoice in the Lamb.

> *For he counteracts the Devil, who is death,*
> *by brisking about the life.*
> *For in his morning orisons he loves the sun*
> *and the sun loves him.*

Smart must have thought that if he put on a good enough show, he might actually compel all of London to join his devotional drama. Together, their voices would soar to heaven as one grand polyhymnic never-ending song of praise, echoing the one Smart already heard in his head: a song of praise for the Creator which all creation, by its very existence, sings.

They locked him up in a private madhouse in Bethnal Green in 1759.

For being a public nuisance.

For giving the Lord away for free.

For being grateful.

> *For he purrs in thankfulness, when God*
> *tells him he's a good cat*

That little excitable man, that gregarious, madcap, theatrically-bent Kit Smart, former "Scholar of The University"—who loved nothing more than to see and hear and smell and taste and touch and cover himself with the Maker in all of His manifestations—was confined to a tiny cold stone room for four years.

Him and his cat Jeoffry.

It was there at Bethnal Green that Smart wrote the oracular poem *Jubilate Agno*. After his release, he lived in poverty and obscurity. His family deserted him while he was confined. He died in a debtor's jail.

I wrote my master's thesis about Kit Smart, his poem *Jubilate Agno*, and his remarkable feline companion. I wrote it during the so-called "height" of the Reagan years, when one was expected to be pugnaciously cheerful about intolerance, greed, cowardice, and stupidity.

In graduate school, you are expected to obsess over some obscure figure and try to elevate them—and, not incidentally, yourself—to national importance. Maybe that's what I was doing then—and, with this essay, maybe that's what I am doing now. But the image of little Kit Smart locked in his room for four years, playing catch-the-cork with his cat and writing his personal testament of gratitude for God's glory—remains a haunting one.

Maybe that's all any of us can hope for after the ravages of this winter, after the ravages of this century. A little room. A little cat or dog or African pygmy hedgehog or whatever creature suits us.

So long as it reminds us to be grateful that we are all wreathed in the living fire.

No matter what.

> *For the electrical fire is the spiritual substance, which God sends from heaven to sustain the bodies of man and beast.*

Dreams I'm Never Gonna See

Skydivers and RV Drivers

My Dad told me that when he turned sixty-five, he was going to celebrate his retirement from the construction industry ... by taking up skydiving.

My father-in-law informed me that when *he* turned sixty-five, he would sell their house of twenty-eight years ... then buy an RV and just drive around the country.

These men were not joking. Their generation—Depression-born, goal-oriented, and fiercely secretive about their heartfelt desires—doesn't kid around when it comes to retirement.

RETIREMENT. Ah, that tantalizing brass ring, that holiest of grails. Now for them so close ... so maddeningly close.

To my father, I could have responded as—well, as he would have responded to me. First the *longggg* pause; the slow labored breathing, followed by a sigh matched only by the last gasp of a beached whale. Then the dubious statement of resignation and acceptance: "Well, if that's what you really want to do, and you've considered all the pros and cons of such a stupid stunt ... ."

To my father-in-law, I could have responded as a typical son-in-law by offering cheerful praise for his Great Escape plans, followed by some subtle comments about the difficulties that lie ahead for my generation—and those that lie ahead for anyone attempting to live in a 50-foot metal Kleenex box riding on little donut wheels so thin and so mortal.

I don't recall what my reply was to these notions of theirs. A coughed obscenity, maybe, or some mumbled false pleasantries which, I'm sure, were misconstrued as tokens of my support and approval.

Given the nature of Social Security, they know that they will have my support, financially speaking.

But will they ever have my approval?

NO! Nothing doing! Who do they think they are? Have they no shame? No sense of propriety? No sense of limitations? What about all that talk of responsibility and "building bridges" and all the rest of those Eagle Scout/Mickey Mantle/Happy Trails horseshit platitudes that they force-fed my generation? Oh yes, there's the "life's grand paradox," right? The child now caring for the parent? To hell with that. Why should I support, nay, enthusiastically *approve* of the reckless and irresponsible acts of my retiring elders—just because they are my retiring elders? Uh-uh. I mean, there they go, flinging themselves out of airplanes, lurching about the backroads and interstates, blocking the flow of our lives, squandering their hoarded capital and national resources, demanding discounts and bullying our elected officials with the sheer size and weight of their amassed savings and medical needs.

No way. Not doing it.

Then I got this videotape in the mail. From my Dad.

Senile old dumbbell. He knows I don't have a TV.

I borrowed a TV and VCR and sat down to watch the tape by myself.

"The Old Man's 65th Birthday Jump – May 6, 1995," it was titled. *Ha!* I caught myself smiling despite myself.

That crazy old man. He did it.

Hmmmph! Don't *even* want him to talk about the wild things I've done. Jumping out of a perfectly good airplane at 15,000 feet! Falling at over 120 mph! Beats me, Daddy-o. You win again.

I expected to chortle and hoot and holler with derision throughout the video. But when I saw him all suited up and ready to board the aircraft—something happened to me.

He was dressed up in this big floppy blue flight suit, you know? He had on brand-new white Reeboks and a big bulbous helmet and tinted goggles, see? He was all trussed up with nylon webbing and support straps.

He waddled when he walked, just like ... like ...

My throat closed up.

Then he was sitting *(too damn close!)* by the plane's open hatchway, where the laser-blue sky poured through, and stretched out below him was the remote mosaic of greenery and black-blue bodies of water that is central Florida and—

Jesus! He and one of the instructors were sucked out of the plane, the two of them turning a tandem somersault and then shrinking before the camera's focus in the blink of my watering eye. They were gone.

My heart thudded loudly. "He's nuts," I muttered weakly.

But then there he was again. The cameraman skydiver was a few feet in front of him, moving around him fluid and easy, like a waterbug. Dad was lashed to the instructor pancaked on top of him. Under a dazzling sun that glanced diamonds off the camera's lens, they hurtled together through the sky, bound by nylon and karma—two tiny colorful pixies trapped forever in God's own blown-glass Christmas ornament.

I got furious and dry-mouthed and screamed raggedly at the TV.

"YOU FOOL! YOU JERK! YOU WOULDN'T EVEN LET ME PULL YOU WATERSKIING!"

And then I started to cry.

Because he looked like … a *baby!* I mean, he looked so damn helpless! The speed of his fall forced a huge infantile grin on his face, the wind flapped and blubbered his lips, and it jerked at his arms and legs, making them move in that shaky hesitant way a toddler moves.

What is this? I choked. *What's going on here? Is this life's grand paradox happening here?*

Who the hell was this mad brave baby in the floppy blue jumpsuit?

Father of four? Korean War vet? Tired and angry bricklayer, stonemason, concrete finisher, contractor, and victim/hero against Big Business? An American Sisyphus who toiled a lifetime, rolling that stone uphill and, when he finally got that sucker to stay there, celebrated by flinging himself down from the mount of the gods?

And why did he look so happy?

That was the most painful question that I formulated, out loud, while watching my newborn retiree rocketing toward the ground, rolling and spinning and grinning and waving and pointing down to his destination either final or immediate.

And that is the question I would like to put to all those brave old skydivers and RV drivers.

That's okay. You don't have to tell me. Whatever the reason, and I guess, whatever the cost—it's OK by me.

You have my approval.

Just want you grown-ups to be happy, you know?

In Praise of Polish Cavalry

The recent celebration of the 50th anniversary of VE Day brought to mind my neighbor, Mr. Beamon, and his favorite expression of futility.

Mr. Beamon was a WWII veteran, an ex-tanker who had fought in Tunisia. He was hot-tempered, foul-mouthed, and hypervigilant of his property—which meant that he and his quarter-acre lot were the most compelling attractions in our neighborhood. Kids would come from miles away just to ride their Stingrays through his lawn and receive those astonishingly inventive curses for which Mr. Beamon was known.

Kids called him "Beamon the Demon."

And the only *printable* nickname he gave back to the kids who tormented him was "miserable bedbugs."

He liked me, though. I'm still not sure why. Maybe it was because from time to time I helped him defend his property against invading insects and weeds. Or maybe it was because he never identified me as one of the Stingray Marauders who kept pedaling through his dewy lawn at dusk.

Whatever the reason, Mr. Beamon actually talked to me. "Hey ya little turd—c'mere" was his usual invitation to an afternoon of forking out dandelions and crabgrass, burning tentworm nests and anthills, or lining the borders of his yard with flaked stone and chipped bricks, or other anti-bicycle traps. And drinking lots of warm Fanta Orange Soda.

He was loaded with colorful expressions. But even then I realized that most of them were best reserved for extreme circumstances. Like weeding. Like killing bugs.

But his favorite expression was "like Polish cavalry."

He said that all the time. He said it when his squirrelcage pushmower could not keep up with the lush growth near the septic tank and the willows in the backyard. He said it when he shot a large dog with his pelletgun and the dog just looked at his own flank, looked at Mr. Beamon, and then continued to disburden himself under Mr. Beamon's sugar maple. He said it when he broke his snowshovel and had to borrow one from my Dad, and then he broke that one, too.

It seemed to me that he saved "like Polish cavalry" for times of defeat. Yet I never ever heard him speak those words in anger. He uttered them solemnly, almost reverently. He'd nod his head after he'd said them, in silent affirmation of the superior forces that were impervious to his efforts or otherwise beyond his control.

He never offered an explanation. And I never asked him what it meant. I knew he wasn't Polish. I could tell it wasn't a joke. But I didn't know exactly *what* it was.

It was a curious expression then, and it is so even today, I suppose. Had he resorted to some other more popular expression of futility such as "like a snowball's chance in hell," "like a fart in a whirlwind," or "like a one-legged man in an ass-kickin' contest"—the meaning would have been clearer. *Reality defends its borders, kid. It don't suffer trespassers lightly.*

But with "like Polish cavalry"—what lesson of human frailty was he trying to teach? What commentary on cultural limitations and boundaries was he offering?

This much is possible:

In September 1939, Polish cavalry regiments responded to German armored columns that were sweeping across the flat plains of their homeland. That impressed Mr Beamon, because the cavalry units *charged* the tanks—and were butchered within minutes.

This much is conjecture:

Mr. Beamon was *so* impressed that when the Japanese bombed Pearl Harbor, he joined up with an armored unit, so to better the odds of returning home alive to the States.

And this much is certain:

That he lost both his arms to a German 88mm shell that found the mark on his tank. The rest of his crew died from various injuries: Spalled metal or exploding rivets piercing their bodies; burning fuel, lubricating oil or molten aluminum broiling them into eternity. He didn't know which.

"I never knew what hit me," he would say over and over again to a very impressionable boy who both pitied and envied a man who could snap snowshovel handles with his mechanical hooks.

And now a very impressionable man sits here wondering what exactly *was* the lesson to be learned from the fate of the Polish cavalrymen.

Was it …

Reality defends its borders?

Don't go up against panzers ridin' a pony, kid?

Machines are better than people, kid? But they play hell with snowshovel handles.

I envision what it must have been like for the Polish cavalrymen. The hot sticky sun of September in their faces. Horses' ears pricking, hooves stamping. The malty smell of horse sweat and the acrid smell of human fear sweat mingling with the tang of oiled leather boots and saddles.

The dull rumbling of engines and the chatter and squeak of steel tracks on steel wheels coming towards them … .

My God! They knew. They *knew.*

The most poignant expression of futility of the 20th century: We will all someday, somewhere, somehow be matched against machines.

And the outcome will be called progress. Or efficiency. Or technological superiority. Or the Third Wave.

But let us charge them while we can, anyway.

And let us praise the Polish cavalry.

GENERAL ⊛ ELECTRIC
COMPANY
SPACE DIVISION

J. C. CASTLE
GENERAL MANAGER
GROUND SYSTEMS DEPARTMENT

P. O. BOX 2500
DAYTONA BEACH, FLORIDA 32015
A/C 904 258-2238

December 8, 1978

Brian Knopp
DeLand High School
4 Domingo Road
DeLand, Florida 32720

Dear Brian:

It is my pleasure to send you the attached photograph as a memento of your participation in the General Electric Company's Centennial Essay Contest.

I would like to thank you for entering the contest and congratulate you again as one of the winners.

Best regards,

J.C. Castle

Attachment

76

Building the Perfect Mouse

OR

How Pinocchio Gave Abe Lincoln His Chance

In 1879, Thomas Alva Edison invented the light bulb. In 1978, while a senior in high school, I wrote a winning essay about him for General Electric's Centennial of Light Exposition the following year. As a finalist in the Centennial of Light contest, I won a fifty dollar savings bond, which was the primary incentive for my essay. Yet I also received an invitation to tour both GE and the central Florida military-industrial corporations of my choice, and a special invitation to see the "real magic" of Walt Disney World.

I was overwhelmed. I had only wanted to pay for a broken window in my Dad's truck.

Like other tours, trips, pilgrimages or journeys to the underworld, the tour of Disney World started off with speeches. One of the speakers humorously praised Edison for his tenacity and ingenuity in the face of eccentricity. Another speaker admired Edison's pioneer spirit, and lamented how primitive things really were back in 1879, yet rejoiced how different things are today, now that we have learned enough about our world through science and technology to build our future today. Finally, a member of Walt Disney Productions spoke mostly about their plans for EPCOT, an Experimental Prototype Community Of Tomorrow undertaken in the spirit of inventive pioneers such as Thomas Alva Edison and Walter Elias Disney.

Up until this speech, I had regarded this whole Centennial of Light Exposition with the sort of bemused detachment befitting a high school student who was not science-oriented and who was not about to admit it as long as savings bonds, free meals, and out-of-school field trips were available. The seminars and industrial PR tours were interesting insofar as they were rich sources of information for the bullshit artist status I coveted at seventeen. But I really did want to find out how Edison, high-tech wizardry, and Mickey Mouse all fit together.

The speaker from Walt Disney Productions gave me the border to the puzzle. After a few minutes of hat-doffing to Edison, he explained how EPCOT, a "living laboratory" for city planning of the future, was a logical extension of the philosophy and technological innovation behind all of Walt Disney's efforts. The philosophy, in a phrase, was "Be Ahead of the Problem," and technological innovation complemented that philosophy. The man then spoke movingly about Walt Disney's lifelong concern for the quality of *family* life—he would repeatedly emphasize the word with both hands opened outward in the orator's gesture of invitation and inclusion—and about how Disney World applied state-of-the-art technology to solve the problem of how to entertain *the family*. The speaker went on to suggest that EPCOT would be a similar application to solve the problem of how to best house many families in an urban setting.

Then he launched into a description of the various presentations and pavilions: Journey into Imagination; The American Adventure; World of Motion; World Showcase. Using certain Disney World attractions as analogs, he made it quite clear that EPCOT's development depended on Disney World's success as a controlled entertainment and communications environment, an environment which could inspire visitors or "guests," as they were called, to "embrace the future with optimism"—365 days of the year. He ended his speech with a little whimsy: he quoted an architect who said how wonderful it would be if our troubled cities could be saved by a mouse!

Pretty heady stuff, I thought. *So Walt like to fool with gadgets, just like Edison, huh? Walt Disney wanted to build the perfect mouse. No, wanted to build the perfect house. For a mouse? For a mouse family? The best laid plans of ... what are we, men or ... ?*

The sound of applause broke my reverie. I got up and followed the seminar crowd as it shuffled out of the convention hall. As we bunched up in the lobby, I noticed that the crowd seemed subdued, introspective. People walked around aimlessly, avoiding conversation, lost in their respect and admiration for Walt Disney. Perhaps for his savior Mouse as well.

The crowd was soon divided into several smaller groups, and each group was given a particular time and destination at which their two-hour tour of Disney World would begin. At the end of the tour, we were to be given complimentary coupon books for the rides and attractions, which we could enjoy until the closing banquet.

My group started with a look at how Disney World kept itself so clean. We were told how Disney World is one of the most efficient, pollution-free, self-governing communities in the world. Our guide gave a brief history of the construction of the theme park, of the need for absolute control over construction, maintenance, energy consumption, and waste disposal, in order to have the kind of efficient and pleasant atmosphere that Walt Disney had in mind. He told us about Reedy Creek Improvement District, the governing agency which wrote its own building codes in order to implement that type of absolute control; about the wonderful AVAC garbage disposal system which sucks garbage from hidden receptacles and hurls it 60 mph down polished tubes that lead to the fully-automated compacting station at the edge of The Magic Kingdom; about the incineration plant which cleans itself with waste water that is itself purged and recycled naturally through a "Living Farm" of plants and trees; about the energy plant that converts its waste heat into chilled water which in turn is used for air conditioning in many of the buildings at Disney World.

As if the guide sensed my sudden irrational fear of accidentally falling into one of the subtle garbage bins and ending up as waste heat or air conditioning, he looked directly at me and reassured that all systems were integrated into a network of computers, fiber optic sensors, and TV monitors, the likes of which were not to be found anywhere else in the world. He added that Disney World's dedicated maintenance staff was second to none, as well. "We can't forget the 'human element' which gives

Disney World its unique atmosphere," he reminded, and then he went on to describe this "element." By day, costumed sanitation workers patrol the streets, looking for litter; by night, legions of maintenance crews swarm over the deserted Magic Kingdom, hosing down every street, scraping up every wad of gum, replacing every trampled bush and uprooted patch of sod, repainting every smudged, nicked, or dulled surface they see.

Getting back to my irrational fears, the guide began to talk about the safety of Disney World: The phenomenal safety record for all the rides and attractions, the almost 100% occupancy for the hotels, and so on. And to show us how it was done, he led us to Cinderella's Castle—and then *below* it.

Our guide led us through a pair of security doors which were monitored by TV cameras, then down a ramp which opened into a maze of long corridors called "Utilidors." Ribbons of fluorescent light cast a greenish hue on the rough concrete walls which had direction signs on them. The machine-finished concrete floors were spotless except for rubber marks left by the little service carts which zoomed around continuously. Overhead, white metallic tubes, conduit pipes, and ventilation boxes rested on metal braces with rollers. The walls hummed slightly, the floors echoed the scuff of our heels, the service carts beeped and whirred down the corridors, and heavy metal fire doors clicked open and clanged shut. There was constant motion, constant activity, but it was the kind of activity that made you feel lonely, like watching a light beacon revolve around and around.

According to the signs, we were now underneath Main Street. Our guide led us through two huge green fire doors and into a room filled with computer cabinets. This was the central control room for the DACS computer, according to our guide. He then introduced us to a tired-looking little man who apparently ran the place. The little man told us how the service basement or underground infrastructure gave maintenance crews access to electric, sewage, and heating lines; it contained employee cafeterias, management offices, costume and small equipment repair shops—and of course, the main computer terminal.

Furthermore, as the little man explained, the "underground" allows employees to travel to their designated area swiftly and unobtrusively. Thus the Disney characters like Mickey Mouse and Donald Duck can truly appear "anywhere we want them to—like Magic!" Likewise, maintenance and security crews can emerge from hidden entrances inside the attractions themselves so as not to alarm the guests with their presence and consequently ruin the atmosphere. Our regular guide added that in case of an accident, medical technicians can move quickly to the scene, while Disney characters simultaneously deploy nearby to distract the guests and keep them from hampering first aid procedures.

I asked my first and only question of the day: How did they know when and where an accident happened? Both men smiled; the tired-looking little man looked less tired and said "Ah, that is a good question," and then made a sweeping gesture towards the glowing blinking clicking cabinets all around us. "This is how we know—and how we keep accidents from happening in the first place."

The now not-so-tired-looking little man answered my question in depth. Just as all the power, waste disposal, and other utility systems were integrated into a communication network of computers and sensors, so, too, were all of the attractions, vending booths, and employee deployment areas. Practically every aspect of Disney World is controlled, synchronized, and monitored in order to, in his words, "provide our guests with the cleanest, safest and most enjoyable entertainment available in the world today."

A colleague asked if Disney World spied on the guests themselves, like in their hotel rooms? Both men laughed and the little man added that such spying most certainly would *not* increase the guests' enjoyment of Disney World. "Disney World loses millions of dollars a year in retail theft. Sometimes we know who did what, but we respect the privacy and rights of our guests too much to confront them with the very technology that makes the Magic of Disney World possible."

Someone else from the group asked the little man for a demonstration of this technological Magic. He obliged by scurrying over to a metal cabinet and pointing to the slowly moving spools of magnetic tape. "Here is the Haunted Mansion," he said. Then he went down a short hallway, stepping over a place where some floor tiles had been removed, revealing bundles of heavy power lines and smaller wiring, and pointed to some women seated at a control desk which was studded with lights and switches. The women were watching TV monitors. "And this is the Haunted Mansion." On one screen I saw several people laughing and screaming in a small corridor that seemed to be closing in on them. On the other screen all I saw were greenish-white humanoid shapes, and then suddenly a bright-yellow dot flared up and began to move up and down in front of one of the humanoid blobs.

"That is a thermal image," he explained. "Someone has just lit up a cigarette in the area of the dining room stage of the Mansion; security has been alerted, and a tape recording is now being broadcast in the area in three languages reminding guests that smoking is forbidden." The little man told us how the music, the special effects, and the security measures are all synchronized by these computers and monitored by "Imagineers." If a child were to somehow fall out of one of the cars, pressure pads on either side of the track would stop the ride itself, delay the special effects within the immediate viewing area of the car in question, and a voice recording would advise guests to please stay in their seats at all times for the safety and enjoyment of everyone.

The room erupted in questions from the group. How frequent are accidents involving the rides? How dangerous are the attractions, anyway? Is everything monitored in Disney World? Before he could answer, our guide stepped in and shoved his watch in our faces, muttered pleasantly, and hustled away like the White Rabbit from Wonderland, and we hurried after him.

After walking down several more Utilidors, we were surprised by the sight of Balloo the Bear and Chip of Chip'n Dale fame walking towards us. They were carrying their huge costume heads under their arms, and the human faces were sweaty, their eyes strangely empty of expression, like coal miners' eyes. Our guide waved to them but they just trudged past us. He explained that being a Disney character was a demanding but rewarding experience. He promised that the folks working in the costume shop could tell us more about that experience.

We walked through another pair of green fire doors and were greeted by five of the Seven Dwarves' heads sitting on a stand. A lively woman in a green lab coat greeted us and proceeded to tell us all about the costume shop. Since there are thousands of costumed figures in Disney World—from themed restaurant workers to the Disney characters themselves—each costume is coded and logged into a computer that can track the location and status of each and every piece of the ensemble. As for the character costumes, the large plastic heads and animal costumes are cumbersome and somewhat hot but not unreasonably so. They are equipped with vision and respiration screens, and the costumes can be removed quickly for emergencies and so on … .

Then she told us about the unique difficulties of being a character. Characters cannot talk to anyone for any reason once they leave the underground. Characters in any stage of costume dress are confined to designated underground areas when they are not performing. Even restaurant, gift shop, and maintenance employees are not allowed to wear any Disney-related apparel outside of the theme park boundaries, unless the clothing was classified as retail. Characters have strict behavior codes, and they are expected to be ready at a moment's notice to give 200% to the guests.

Some characters have been seriously injured by unruly guests or by accidents caused by their unfamiliarity with the costume or with the stairwells leading out of the underground. One character, she related, whose costume was designed to resemble a bear that walks around on its hands, tripped and fell while above ground. Because the actor inside was not allowed to speak, he could not stop the guests from repeatedly standing him "upside down" on his head. He was badly injured as a result. She also told us how several of the smaller characters such as Mickey Mouse and Chip'n Dale have to be extra careful about being the victims of guests' excessive enthusiasm which could lead to "mishandling" them.

The lively woman reminded us that "Disney World's characters are so charmingly convincing that it is easy to forget that there are real people inside of them!"

This remark caused several people to chuckle appreciatively, including our guide, who interjected that "on the other hand, Disney World has human characters so real, it is hard to believe that they are not real people!" He was referring to the culmination of Disney Magic: The Audio-Animatronics. We were in for a real treat at the next stop on our tour, he promised, because we would have the "opportunity of a lifetime" to see an Audio-Animatronic "up close and personal."

We walked down another Utilidor, through still yet another pair of green fire doors, and into what looked like a typical electronics repair shop. Spools of wire lay everywhere, along with metal mounting brackets, electrician's tools, and oscilloscope boxes all piled atop movable carts. The room had the smell of heated plastic. The Imagineers dressed in white lab coats were studying computer printouts, clicked away on computer keyboards, glanced occasionally at the several large clocks mounted on the walls. Nothing looked particularly "once in a lifetime" about the place. Just a lot of electronic gear, technicians, and an ape on one of the carts.

An ape on one of the carts! I pushed ahead of the group for a better look, while the tour guide and one of the technicians looked on. The ape had a human's flesh-colored yet cartoon shaped ape face, but the body was clear plastic, through which a shiny metal skeleton of articulating rods and slender hydraulic rams could be seen when not obscured by the ape's electronic circulatory system of multicolored bundled wires. I remember seeing this character before—the fully furred version—in one of the themed attractions. At that time, I thought it looked silly and harmless.

But now, gawking at the ape's rather human leer and inert robot body, I felt wary and uneasy. It was a man, an animal, and a machine, all at once. It was both alive and dead. Like people who visit wax museums or stare at particularly life-like mannequins, I was convinced that it moved, or at least seemed to grow more animated the longer I stood motionless and stared it.

The guide stepped to the cart and introduced one of the Imagineers working there. The Imagineer walked up to the cart and patted the ape on the head (*did it just glance at the Imagineer? Absurd. But I swear … .)* and introduced the ape as one of the musicians for the Mickey Mouse Review. The ape was in for repairs, he explained, which normally would take place either at a much larger repair shop at Disney World, or at WED (Walter Elias Disney) Enterprises located in Glendale, California. But they left the ape here so we could see him as part of our tour. The Imagineer spoke briefly about WED and MAYPO (short for *Mary Poppins)*, the two organizations that design and manufacture, respectively, most of the attractions at both Disneyland and Disney World. He added that both organizations benefit from the technologies developed by GE, RCA and Monsanto, whose corporate sponsorship helped developed several of Disney World's themed villages and attractions.

The Imagineer told us the history of Audio-Animatronics, which he jokingly referred to as the "true story of how Pinocchio became a real boy." As an animator, Walt Disney was fascinated with the various techniques of approximating or reproducing "real life" as a form of entertainment. His willingness to try new technologies made his cartoons and live-action films highly successful. With full-length cartoons such as *Pinocchio,* for example, Walt's animators used dolls as models for their drawings. This wasn't particularly innovative in itself—rotoscoping using human figurines and live action films had been around for years—but it sparked Walt's interest in creating three-dimensional characters that could be controlled as precisely as cartoon figures could, i.e., movement by movement, frame by frame.

In 1955, WED Imagineers used an activation technique, which NASA would later improve upon to launch its rockets, to control the mechanical figures that Walt had been working on in secret since 1945. Using sound impulses on magnetic tape—music, speech, special effects— to control electronic/hydraulic/pneumatic robots, WED Imagineers had brought Pinocchio to life, so to speak. Walt Disney finally had his "living cartoons:" Audio-Animatronics, or "AA's," for short.

The first successful application of Audio-Animatronics was Disneyland's "Tiki Birds." But the first real demonstration of the AA's extraordinary versatility and lifelike quality was at the 1964 World's Fair in New York, where audiences were awed by the AA figure of Abraham Lincoln, the sitting, standing, talking, and gesturing 16th President and star of the Illinois pavilion.

At this point, the Imagineer stopped for a minute, smiled and shook his head. "Boy," he said, "did we have trouble with him at first!" He went on to relate how potentially destructive AA figures like Lincoln can be; how their hydraulic limbs have several hundred pounds of mechanical energy which can be activated accidentally by lightning storms or static electricity; how Imagineers working with AA's have to make sure the AA figures and themselves are grounded at all times; how the Lincoln AA had injured several workers before being brought under control; how Imagineers have to be careful about a fire breaking out in the AA work room, because even if a small fire were to start, the workers would be automatically locked in the room while the temperature quickly dropped to well below zero in order to protect the AA's circuitry.

He also explained some isolated incidents where workers suffered from psychological stress at seeing these figures suddenly "come alive" when they had been supposedly shut down. "To have an AA figure turn and look at you while you are working on it—it's an unforgettable experience."

Then the Imagineer pointed to the ape resting on the cart and advised "some of the plastic compounds used for the AA figures actually produce oils, just like human skin does."

I stopped watching the ape. I couldn't deal with the prospect of a sweating robot.

The Imagineer talked about the Hall of Presidents, with which most of the tour group was familiar. "It's wonderful to see Abe Lincoln talking to Dwight Eisenhower—to Jimmy Carter, even!"

He waxed prophetic, predicting that AA figures would eventually be much more than "perfect actors who never miss a cue, or argue with the director, or go on strike." They might also carry out maintenance and service-oriented tasks at Disney World. "After all," he shrugged, "AA's don't mind pushing a broom all day long."

Our guide nodded rapidly in agreement, and asked us if we had any quick questions. Someone asked how much the AA's cost to build, someone else asked something entirely technical-sounding—I wasn't listening anymore. I was drifting away from the group, away from that damn ape that kept mocking me with that simian/human knowing grin of his.

I backed out of the room and stood in the Utilidor. I had trouble tying my shoe. All this talk of animation/robots/apes made me terribly self-conscious of performing even simple actions.

Abe Lincoln got his chance—from Pinocchio. The American Dream: from puppet to cartoon to real boy to President of the United States.

My mind was racing. The puzzle was filling in nicely. Pinocchio couldn't tell lies very well. Honest Abe didn't tell lies at all.

Ole Abe Lincoln could split rail posts all day long, so the story goes. Walt Disney believed it. Pinocchio helped him prove it. Now AA Lincoln's constituents could push brooms all day long.

I watched Donald Duck and his nephews waddle down the Utilidor. Those stupid shoes they had to wear would make anyone waddle.

Two security guards in quaint 19th century costume police uniforms with rows of brass buttons and shoe spats wheeled their little cart around the corner of the Utilidor, with Pluto sitting behind them.

"Perfect actors who never miss a cue, or argue with the director, or go on strike."

Far down the corridor were two people dressed like sanitation workers from the 1890s, one of them pulling a little "honey dipper" bucket for cleaning up after real horses that were nowhere to be found.

"After all, AA's don't mind pushing a broom all day long."

Something was terribly wrong with the puzzle.

My tour group came out of the AA repair shop and assembled in the Utilidor. I joined them. We walked back to Main Street and Cinderella's Castle.

"Cinderella do your work!" screamed her stepmother in the movie.

"After all, AA's don't mind pushing a broom all day long."

We emerged from the underground. Everyone praised the infrastructure, the AA technology, and Walt Disney, in general. But there was one big collective sigh of relief when we could feel the bright warm sun again.

Our guide distributed coupon books for the attractions and rides and reminded us about the evening banquet. Then he demurely asked us not to take advantage of Disney World's hospitality, which had allowed us to see "how it all works."

"Please don't spoil the Magic for the other guests!" he pleaded.

All present agreed not to, Mouseketeer's honor.

Well. The Magic was spoiled for *me*. It wasn't like I had just seen the circus clown without his makeup, or the magician's false-bottomed box. On the contrary, such revelations often reassured. There was comfort in knowing that underneath the garish makeup was an ex-alcoholic who needed the gig for child support payments, or that the magician didn't really saw women in half for applause.

I didn't feel any better knowing that underneath a character's pounds of vinyl and cloth was a human being who couldn't cry out when hurt, couldn't talk in the light of day, couldn't be anywhere except for a computer-designated right place at the computer-designated right time.

I didn't feel better knowing that Disney World would watch me smoke pot, steal a stuffed Winnie-the-Pooh, or drop dead of a heart attack—and then send out Tigger to keep the guests from seeing cops or paramedics take me away down to the underground.

And I certainly did not feel better knowing Audio-Animatronics could sweat, crush an Imagineer, or push a broom all day long.

Edison. EPCOT. Pinocchio. Lincoln.

"Be Ahead of the Problem."

Something was really really wrong with the puzzle.

Disney World—"An environment which could inspire visitor's to embrace the future with optimism—365 days a year."

Who's afraid of Disney World? *Tra-la-la-la-la!*

I stared at Liberty Square. For the first time I realized that the buildings were built to different scales. The windows, shutters—all the building trim details—got smaller as you went up, making the buildings appear taller and bigger than they really were.

Some Colonial sanitation men in tri-cornered hats strolled by, picking up wrappers from Liberty Bell chocolates. The "human element" at it again.

"AFTER ALL, AA'S DON'T MIND PUSHING A BROOM ALL DAY LONG!"

That phrase had established itself. It kept nagging me. It made me angry. It reminded me of something, it warned me of something. But I couldn't figure out exactly what that "something" was.

I walked around in the theme park, thinking about brooms. I was surprised to find myself heading towards the major attractions without intending to. The motion of the monorails and the people-movers, the layout of the streets, the position of the buildings, even the appearance of Disney characters—all acted like magnets, drawing guests like me this way and that. I had simply been sucked into the flow of people. Even when I tried to go against the flow, I found myself following a color or a building design or the provocative waltzing of a Disney character and right back in the flow I was. Like Magic.

I went to Space Mountain, the Haunted Mansion, the Pirates of the Caribbean, and the Hall of the Presidents. The knowledge that I was being watched, that I was being controlled where and when to look by the very design of the rides themselves—didn't bother me at all. Nor did the repetitive sound tracks celebrating corporate sponsorship and the inevitability of capitalistic perfection: *"R-C-A leads the way! Leads the way!" "It's a Small World after all!" "Live for tomorrow—TODAY!"* And the Audio-Animatronics were once again their delightfully ingenious, entertaining selves, eager to please, to imitate, to educate, to—

"PUSH A BROOM ALL DAY LONG!"

Fantastic.

"*FANTASIA!*" I screamed aloud, startling not a few guests who were leaving the Hall of the Presidents.

That's why I kept thinking about brooms! In the Disney movie *Fantasia*, Mickey Mouse is damn near killed by robot brooms!

It was in "The Sorcerer's Apprentice." Mickey uses the wizard's magical hat to get out of doing his chores. He brings a broom to life and commands it to fill a large cistern with water. The broom mechanistically picks up two empty buckets and starts to work. Pleased with his success, Mickey dozes off and dreams of controlling the motion of the stars and planets themselves.

But Mickey's ambition gets the best of him: he creates an enormous ocean wave which almost knocks him off his mountain perch, thus ending his dream. He awakes to find the wizard's cavern flooded by the diligent broom. When Mickey tries to stop the automaton with an axe, it splits into thousands of identical brooms, each armed with buckets of water. Only the wizard's return saves Mickey from disaster. Chastened by the wizard's spanking, Mickey goes about his work.

I was thrilled to have remembered the movie! And clearly there was something Mickey-esque about designing PERFECT ACTORS WHO NEVER MISS A CUE, about three-dimensional cartoons who wouldn't mind PUSHING A BROOM ALL DAY LONG: those dangerous Audio-Animatronics.

But not so fast … .

Because Mickey became an Audio-Animatronic. So did Pinocchio. So did thirty-nine American presidents. *They* are the brooms who have split and multiplied. And that is not a bad thing, according to Walter Elias Disney.

Because the lesson he wanted to impart from "The Sorcerer's Apprentice" was *not* "Never let a broom do what a mouse should be doing."

No. The lesson was "Never put on a wizard's hat, little Mouse!"

And so we human "characters" will not cry out through the pounds and pounds of vinyl and acetate, we "brooms" will not miss a wad of gum, and we "guests" will not fail to move street by street, attraction to attraction—controlled frame by controlled frame—through the three-dimensional cartoon that is Disney World.

Because we "EMBRACE THE FUTURE WITH OPTIMISM."

Because the wizards with their hats have promised that we will not be rats in a rat race.

We will be mice in urban Magic Kingdoms.

The urban Magic Kingdoms will be clean, safe, and have so much to see.

We will love them.

Acknowledgments

No book is possible—let alone the successful commission of a federal crime like 47 USC § 333 (*No person shall willfully or maliciously interfere with or cause interference to any radio communications of any station licensed or authorized by or under this chapter or operated by the United States Government*)—without good friends caring.

I would like to thank Jeff Rochford a.k.a. "The Rock," Charles Churchill a.k.a. "Charlie the Tuna," and my twin brother Brad Knopp a.k.a. "Thing Two" (hey, I'm nine minutes older, remember?) for their support back in 1981 and for their support now with this project.

Tim "The Ace" Boylan, R.I.P. You're cheering for us wherever you are, I feel it, I know it. You're not in Hell because supposedly nothing is funny there, so you would be kicked out even if you were sent there by mistake.

Susan Rhew's superb book and cover redesign made me like my essays more than when I first wrote them. Writers aren't supposed to admit such things, but it is undeniably true. Monster thanks, Susan!

I am also indebted to Maggie Powell (www.maggiepowelldesigns.com) for the initial design planning and layout consultation for this collection of essays.

Huge messy superabundant gratitude for all the love, support, and marathon patience of Sig "Raging Rooster" Larsen and Linda "Little Dremel" Larsen.

Sheila Jane "Noodle Dog" Pynes showed she is a patroness of all artistic endeavors, no matter how small. Yay!

Finally, a disclaimer. The takeover of KRXY 107.5 (Y108 Lakewood Colorado) in the fall of 1988 by James Kiss was not to my knowledge a copycat takeover. None of the members of ILLO knew him or knew of him prior to his own rash act. WDIZ never mentioned our 1981 takeover on the air or in any other media outlet except for the cryptic reference made by DJ Mick Dolan on the air to the "Rock-n-Roll Commandos from DeLand" on August 6, 1981.

As of July 4, 2024, Mick Dolan had neither responded in substance to solicitations by Jeff Rochford and myself for an interview, nor had he independently offered his recollection of the takeover, in spite of both Jeff and I reaching out to Dolan via Facebook messaging and email numerous times in 2016 and again in 2024.

As for Kiss, he was allegedly an ardent Smiths fan, and Y108's disturbing obsession for narrow playlist Top 40 drove him to desperate measures to improve their playlist rotation. As for Dolan—don't know what his problem is. Sad that such a formerly hip DJ would now refuse to acknowledge, let alone desire to be part of, a fun story about a ridiculous and mercifully benign stunt for which he is uniquely if not solely responsible. DJs like Dolan certainly grow old and forget things and eventually die. But as Bob Seger would argue—rock-n-roll never forgets.

Nor will I.

Brian Lee Knopp
July 4, 2024

About the Author

Brian Lee Knopp is a retired North Carolina private investigator. In 2019, he published the revised 2nd edition of his acclaimed 2009 memoir *Mayhem in Mayberry: Misadventures of a P.I. in Southern Appalachia* (Cosmic Pigbite Press). He created and contributed to the 2012 collaborative novel *Naked Came the Leaf Peeper* (Burning Bush Press). A former professional sheep shearer with an M.A. degree in English Literature from the University of Texas at Austin, Knopp has taught composition at Warren Wilson College and nonfiction writing for the Great Smokies Writing Program at UNC-Asheville. His work has appeared in *Hippocampus Magazine, Stoneboat Journal, WNC Magazine, Now & Then: The Appalachian Magazine, The Great Smokies Review,* and in several regional magazines and anthologies. He lives in Asheville.

"Brian Lee Knopp's eye for character and behavior is so finely tuned he even catches that precise tingling instant baked into Southern Appalachian culture when polite wariness threatens to flash red violent." –Charles Frazier, author of *Cold Mountain*

Even *more* Mayhem in this *revised* 2nd edition!

Mayhem in Mayberry

Misadventures of a P.I. in Southern Appalachia

Brian Lee Knopp

Praise for Mayhem in Mayberry

"Raymond Chandler, author of the finest series of detective novels in the history of the genre, supposedly claimed that he cut his sheets of typing paper into three strips. Each one needed to contain at least one arresting or delightful element—a sharp description, a turn of phrase, an action, an observation. You could chop this book up into strips, and it would surely meet Chandler's requirements. Descriptions crackle with detail, and Brian Lee Knopp's eye for character and behavior is so finely tuned he even catches that precise tingling instant baked into Southern Appalachian culture when polite wariness threatens to flash red violent."

— Charles Frazier, National Book Award winner
and author of *Cold Mountain*

"I love this author and I love this book! Brian Lee Knopp is one of the most natural writers I've ever encountered and he tells this all-too-true story with sinewy wit and sublime grace. There are moments in this book where even Knopp seems filled with amazed disbelief at what he has seen, done and lived through. The best narratives should be windows into worlds that most of us will never encounter, and his world most certainly has been one of strange and intimate marvels. I feel lucky to have been let in."

— Elizabeth Gilbert, author of *Eat, Pray, Love*

"Brian Lee Knopp is an American original, a fearless standup comedian, and a muckraking master of prose, whose *Mayhem in Mayberry: Misadventures of a P.I. in Southern Appalachia* is one of the funniest and most provocative books I've read in years. It's also a breakthrough chronicle of another America, the hilarious underbelly of crime and betrayal, and the still small possibility of redemption. From the back warrens of the hip New South, to the backwoods of the disappearing American frontier, Knopp manages to unfold the secret tales known only to the best private investigator with stunning prose, and powerful insight. This incredible book conjures the spirit of Raymond Chandler's crime classics to the Carolinas, with the brilliant timing and comic narrative of Steve Martin and David Sedaris. *Mayhem in Mayberry* should be an instant classic—an American classic of an undercover private investigator on the frontlines of crime and laugh-out-loud punishment."

— Jeff Biggers, author of *The United States of Appalachia*

"Not since Elmore Leonard's *Maximum Bob* ... have I read a book about a PI that was as funny as it is entertaining, yet Knopp's characters and prose push this book closer to Steinbeck's *Cannery Row* or its sequel *Sweet Thursday*. Read *Mayhem in Mayberry* and rediscover just how much fun a well-written, well-executed book can be."

— *Rapid River*

"A few things make Knopp's memoir of his P.I. days different and worthwhile: his fine writing skills; his love for the Appalachian landscape; his love of the often unintentional humor in the lives of those he meets; a palpable compassion for those caught in bad circumstances they don't deserve ... ."

— *Creative Loafing*

"*Mayhem in Mayberry* is the P.I. book you've been waiting for. Waiting, without even knowing you were waiting, because no one would have thought such a book could be written. Yes, read this if what you are looking for is chase scenes, mad dogs and mountaineers all too fond of shotguns. They are here, presented in striking detail, and with compelling rhythm. Cunning and tenacious, Knopp winds his way through Appalachia in search of people as bent by necessity, as misshapen by the gods, as any creature Odysseus encounters. But P.I. Knopp, like all mythic heroes, is really chasing his own soul, trying to find his way back home. And like Odysseus, he keeps finding that elusive phantom mirrored back to him in the souls of those he hunts."

— David Schenck, Ph.D., poet, Questing Beast,
and author of *Zchenck Among Demons*

www.ingramcontent.com/pod-product-compliance
Lightning Source LLC
Chambersburg PA
CBHW051541120626
46551CB00013B/1323